A PLACE TO LIVE IN YOUR LATER YEARS

Paul B. Maves

RELIGION AND MEDICINE

Glen W. Davidson, Editor

AUGSBURG Publishing House • Minneapolis

A PLACE TO LIVE IN YOUR LATER YEARS

Contents

Foreword

The problems of aging are timely topics not because growing older is new, but because the contexts in which we age,
for most of us, have been radically altered. Both notions of
work and the nature of employment, both the meaning of
family life and its structure, both the styles and quality of
living—all have been altered radically since World War II. As
a consequence, many people have found making decisions
about their later years the most troublesome task of their
lives. At worst this decision making leads to despair. At best
it leads to new opportunities.

A Place to Live in Your Later Years was commissioned for
the Augsburg RELIGION AND MEDICINE SERIES to assist those
who have retired or who expect to retire in the next decade,
to provide some perspective for grown children and other relatives who are concerned about how their loved ones will cope
with aging, and to be usable by church, legal, fiscal, and
health-care professionals who are called upon to advise those
trying to solve the problems of how and where to live in later
life. Like other books in the series, *A Place to Live in Your
Later Years* provides the latest and most reliable information
about problems of how and where to live. The author also

helps the reader draw problem-solving skills from the context of Christian faith. The author was asked to help the reader clarify the problems faced, to identify options that can be considered, and to suggest realistic answers. He has done more as he recommends how to handle the tensions and stresses of these challenges.

Paul Maves is well prepared to write this book. He was born and raised in Nebraska and is now an ordained minister in the Nebraska Annual Conference of the United Methodist Church. He earned his B.D. and Ph.D. degrees at Drew University, where he was a professor of religious education for 17 years. For three years he was Associate Executive Director for a national department of Christian education, and for five years was Director of Field Education and professor of Church Administration at St. Paul School of Theology in Kansas City. He has been a pastor in New York and Vermont. In 1975 he became administrator of a retirement home, Kingsley Manor, in Los Angeles and is now Staff Associate for the Mid-America Resource and Training Center on Aging, directing the National Shepherds Center Development project, which researches living options for the elderly. Dr. Maves is married to Mary Carolyn Hollman. They live in Merriam, Kansas, and have two children. Among other books Paul Maves has written are *Older People and the Church, The Best Is Yet to Be, Understanding Ourselves as Adults,* and *The Church and Mental Illness.*

Glen W. Davidson, Ph.D.
Professor and Chairman
Department of Medical Humanities
Southern Illinois University
    School of Medicine
Springfield, Illinois

Preface

Primarily this book addresses those of us who are aware that changing circumstances will not allow us to keep on living indefinitely where we have been. So we must make a decision about whether to move, and if so, where to move and with whom to live. The circumstance may have occurred already, perhaps with the death of a spouse. Or it may be imminent in the days ahead, perhaps because of failing health or impending retirement.

This book is addressed also to the grown children and other relatives who are involved in the decision-making process either because of personal concern or because of responsibility as next of kin. In any case, usually the entire family is caught up in such decision making. Friends, too, may become involved either by being asked for advice or being tempted to give it unsolicited. In any event, almost none of us will avoid facing this problem sooner or later.

I am one of those who have already gone through this process. My wife and I adjusted to the aging process and changing needs by moving from a four-bedroom suburban house with a large yard to a condominium apartment. Retirement then occasioned another move to a condominium townhouse in another city. As the former administrator of a retirement community and of two associated nursing homes, I am well acquainted with life in both kinds of facilities, life at its best and at its worst.

I have seen my mother go through the process of being twice widowed, of moving from a farm to an apartment in town and then to a retirement hotel in the city. While living at the retirement hotel, she fell and broke a hip, necessitating hospitalization followed by a period of convalescence in a nursing home and then in a boarding home before returning to the hotel. Another fall and additional surgery on her hip forced a move to another nursing home, where she died at age 89. Although she spent much time in the homes of her five children, none of us were able to care for her in our own homes in her last years.

The decisions involved in these moves are not easy. Moving itself is stressful at best. A move that involves "breaking up the home," as the phrase goes, may be even more stressful. But not to decide and not to move may be even worse. On the other hand, there are those who make the decision to move too quickly and who may move when it would be better if they did not.

Always we are challenged to be good stewards of our changing capacities and aware of our changing needs so we can plan well and make the most of the time at our disposal. At the same time, while living as fully as possible, we are called to be responsible for others.

These are the themes to which we will turn our attention in this book as we think together about planning for the future, which includes change. We will discuss these topics from the point of view of a Christian who tries to bring the insights of Christian faith to bear upon some of those trials which put that faith to the test.

1

Confronting Change

Eleanor and Alfreda, both of whom are teachers, neither of whom has ever married, have made their home together for years. (Names used throughout the book have been changed.) Now Eleanor is retired, and Alfreda will retire in two more years. They are asking questions about their future living arrangements. Shall they continue to live in the suburban house with a large yard where they have lived for many years, or shall they move to an apartment? The yard is getting too hard for them to take care of. Hired help is more and more difficult to find. Besides, such help is expensive. Shall they stay in the city where they have worked for many years and have many friends? Or shall they move back to the state where they grew up and where both have a number of relatives? Should they put their names on the waiting list of a highly recommended nearby retirement home which assures life care?

George and his sister Emily have a mother who lives alone in a town halfway across the state. She loves the old family homestead where she brought up her family and where the house is filled with heirlooms. But she is getting frail and forgetful. Her children worry about her. They fear she may fall and not be found for a long time if she could not reach the phone. They fear she may leave the gas jet turned on and asphyxiate herself or leave something on the burner and set the place on fire. The mother adamantly refuses to consider moving. Should they put pressure on her to make a move? And if they were to succeed, where would she live? Their own houses with bedrooms on the second floor are not suitable, and both of them and their spouses go to work during the day.

Charlotte panicked when her husband died after several years of illness. She wanted nothing so much as to get away from the place where they had lived for 40 years. She had never lived alone in her life. She spent the first year "visiting" in the homes of her children. During that time she closed her house, sold most of her furniture, and so burned her bridges to the community in which she had lived so long. But in her children's homes she found little to do. She did not know anyone and found it hard to make friends of her own. She had different interests from those of her children. She felt like a fifth wheel. What should she have done?

For many years since his wife died Edgar has lived alone in a big, old two-story house with a large yard in a once fashionable suburb. He has a dog and two cats for company. He was always handy, skilled in cabinet making, refinishing furniture, and chair caning. Much of the house reflects his handiwork. Now he gets around with great difficulty. He still has his tools and still attempts to cane chairs for those who know about him. But he finds that he has little energy, and his arthritis makes work with his hands painful. The house is becoming run-down. The yard is overgrown. The place is filthy, and the old gentleman is becoming more and more unkempt. For meals he opens cans or warms up frozen dinners. It is hard to get to the store any more. He has no relatives. He is fiercely independent, not wanting to owe anything to any man or woman. So he and the house are decaying together. Should he continue to stay there? Is there something more to life than independence?

Esther, full of energy and pride, lived alone in her house after her husband died. She kept active in the church and had her friends in for bridge. Then within the space of a year her strength waned noticeably. She fell, and her hip was broken. After a stay at the hospital she was transferred to a nursing home for recuperation and rehabilitation. She hated the routine to which she had to conform. She was offended by the lack of privacy and the patronizing air of the attendants. She is frightened by her dependence on others and gets angry when the nurses do not respond quickly to her bell. She misses her old friends, although they too are getting to the point where it would be difficult for them to visit her even if she lived at home. Her hip is mending well. The physical therapy and a good diet are restoring her strength. But there is a real question of whether she will ever be able to care for herself again. Should she stay in the nursing home in the wing for the patients who do not need skilled nursing care? Should she try to hire someone to come in to her own home and take care of her? Should she seek some other kind of living arrangement?

The Ideal and the Reality

Where we will live and how we shall spend our time in our later years are common recurring questions.

There are two prevailing ideal images of living arrangements in the years after retirement. One image is that we will live on until we die in the house that has been home to us for many years, where the children grew up and which is filled with mementos of the past. We will grow full of years, surrounded by family, friends, and familiar things.

The other image is that after retirement we will luxuriate in a resort community where we will be surrounded by opportunities to enjoy ourselves in a life of leisure under the sun, playing golf, fishing, or basking beside a swimming pool. While some people will be able to realize such dreams for a time, most of us will have to consider other arrangements as well. Both of these images require continuing robust health and considerable financial resources.

The time to begin thinking about the possible eventualities is now, no matter what your age or where you are living at present.

The one thing that is certain is that conditions will change. We will change. The community will change. For most of us conditions will change in ways that we cannot now predict with much accuracy. We may want to resist change and to shove the perceptions of change out of our minds, but eventually we will have to confront change. Either we will cope with change openly and make decisions about how we will respond to it, or we will be dragged through change in spite of ourselves. We will take charge of our own lives and grow in the process, or we will let circumstances determine our lives for us and be demeaned.

Many of the changes will force us to make decisions about our living arrangements, about moving from one location to another, about adjusting our way of living to unaccustomed patterns. The accustomed place and the usual ways may no longer be comfortable or safe or viable.

Let's look first at the kinds of change which will require decisions on our part about where to live. Then we will talk about coping with change. After that we will look at alternative possibilities for housing and care.

Changes We May Confront

Let us begin by asking where older Americans in general—those 65 years of age and over—are living now, whom they are living with, and what their situation is.

Of all men 65 and over, 79% are married but only 77% have a spouse present, 13.6% are widowed, and 2.5% are divorced. If we look at the marital status of men 75 years of age and over, we find that 32.3% are widowed.

If we look at the marital situation of women, we see something quite different. Of all women 65 and over, 52.5% are widowed and another 2.6% are divorced. At age 75 69% of the women are widows.

1. Loss of a Spouse

What these statistics tell us is that the loss of a spouse in later maturity is one of the great changes that looms as a real possibility, particularly for women.

Of all the things that can happen to a person, for most people the death of a spouse heads the scale of stress. That loss sets off a chain of events which heighten the original stress even more. When a spouse dies, or when a relative or friend with whom one has been sharing a home dies, the question then comes up, should I move from this place to another? If so, where shall I go?

2. Living Alone

With whom do older people live? According to 1979 statistics 58% of older women and 83% of older men live in family settings. About one-third of all older persons live either alone or with nonrelatives. Four of every ten (42%) older women live alone or with nonrelatives; 17% of older men live alone or with nonrelatives. Only about 5% live in institutions of all kinds. This raises the question of the best place to be when one lives alone, and whether or not it is necessary to live alone.

There is a high probability we will be single in the later years, although most of us will still have family and kinfolk. For generations the family has been expected or required to care for older people. Should we plan on moving in with some of our family? Is this still the best arrangement? Is it what we want? Shall we plan on living alone? Are there other possibilities?

3. Declining Health

Another factor that goes into the making of decisions about where to live is that of changing health and physical capacities. About 40% of all older people experience some limitation in major activities because of a chronic health condition, although only about 20% consider themselves to be functionally impaired or have trouble getting around. For example, a chronic heart condition might not stop an older man from going places, but it might stop him from pushing a lawn mower. So as we get older, the house with three bedrooms, basement, upstairs, attic, and a yard may become more and more difficult to keep unless we can afford to hire all the work done. A disease such as rheumatism may make climbing stairs too much of a chore, just as a tendency to dizziness or unsteadiness on our feet means that we ought not to be climbing ladders. The amount of impairment we experience depends in part on what we believe we should be doing. How do we cope? The longer we live, the more likely we are to experience some disability.

4. Aging Houses

Closely related to this is the fact that 70% of all older people tend to own their homes, and they have lived in them longer than younger people. They do not move as often in later life as in younger life. About half of the older population lives in structures that were built before 1939. What this means is that such houses are less efficient, require more repairs, and cost more to maintain at a time when the persons are less able to do the work themselves and less able to afford hired help. The soaring costs of heating energy-inefficient old houses is an increasingly crucial problem.

5. Changing Neighborhoods

Not only do houses tend to grow old, but so do neighborhoods. Because of the problem of upkeep, neighborhoods occupied largely by older people tend to run down along with the houses. The value of the houses drop, the rents drop, the character of the neighborhood changes. Sidewalks deteriorate and become hazardous. Persons with lower incomes, less able to maintain the property, move in. Sometimes landlords rent out such properties and let them deteriorate as a way of "milking" the equity and profit until they are abandoned. As neighborhoods become poorer, cities tend to decrease their maintenance, so they have poorer garbage collection, less careful street repair and snow removal, and less police protection. The exceptions to this are those affluent neighborhoods which owners have been able to maintain and who have sufficient political power to command the services a neighborhood ought to have.

On a number of occasions I have been given tours of cities with a view to identifying areas in which programs for older people need to be planned and organized. One can almost invariably discern the areas where the older people cluster. The houses are old. They have not been painted as often as needed. The yards are untrimmed and cluttered. Big old trees have made the sidewalks buckle or break. This fact may bespeak the need to develop social policies which prevent the deterioration of neighborhoods rather than have older people leave them. But until that happens, the change in surroundings has to be considered.

As we continue to live in a neighborhood for a number of years, friends and acquaintances may move away or die so that we meet more and more strangers on the street. When children grow up and move out, it becomes more difficult to meet and get acquainted with the newcomers, as persons are no longer brought together through the schools, the Scouts, Little League, and all the other community activities generated by the presence of children. The very fact that children play together tends to bring their parents together.

Even if our grown children live nearby, they have lives of their own. Their involvement in work and community activities may allow them only limited time to spend with us. Their interests and their style of life may diverge from ours.

Studies have shown that older people who continue to live in their old neighborhood generally lose role relationships, and their activities diminish. By contrast, those who move into planned retirement communities tend to increase activities and relationships.

6. Evolving Needs

As we grow older, our needs change too. We may have needed a three- or four-bedroom house when our children were at home, but now that they are gone, we may have unused space to heat and clean, even though we relish the spaciousness and privacy which a larger house affords. The lawn and the garden, once so important for the children to play in, may now lie idle. The flower beds we loved may have become too large to keep weeded.

Or we may not feel comfortable any longer about driving a car, but there is no public transportation near us and taxis are too expensive. We may make more frequent trips to the doctor and the drugstore than we used to, and they are across town. Or we would like to be near a hospital and emergency medical service, but we live out in the country where these things are not to be had.

For those of us who live in the north temperate zone the winters may be more and more of a problem. Once we may have gloried in the winter weather. Now the cold may be getting to our bones, and the snow presents an obstacle to getting out. Some retired persons who can afford it become "snow birds" and go to Southern communities in the winter. Some sell out and move permanently to warmer climates. Most choose to stay in the area where they lived in earlier years. Under what circumstances would a move to a warm climate be warranted?

7. Reduced Income

One more factor in determining where to live and make a home is that after retirement most persons experience a decline in their income, although to some extent this is offset by a decline in expenses. Social Security is the major source of income for most retired Americans. It represents more than half the income for 70% of individual beneficiaries and 50% of couples who are beneficiaries. This may mean that we can no longer afford to keep the large house or rent a large apartment. Common sense seems to suggest looking for a smaller place that does not cost so much.

Communities vary in the cost of living because of the cost of real estate, the tax structure, and accessibility to basic commodities. Retired persons may be worried that they cannot afford to continue living in high-cost areas.

8. Family Concern

Another pressure upon us to move may be our children's increasing uneasiness about us. They may worry because we live alone, and they may be afraid we will be lonely. Perhaps they feel guilty because they cannot get to see us as often as they would like or think they should. They may point out that it is very inconvenient to see us often and look after us where we live and it would be easier for us to move than for them to move. They may be concerned about our safety in a deteriorating neighborhood.

John lived and worked in one of the great cities of the West Coast. His mother lived on the East Coast. He wanted to be able to see her more often. He was assuming more and more responsibility for handling her affairs. Finally he helped her move to a retirement home near his home so he could see her frequently and where she could visit him and his family.

Juanita, 84, lived alone in an apartment where she had spent the last 20 years. Her son lived in the same community. As her strength diminished, she depended more and more on her son and daughter-in-law to come in and clean for her, to transport her, and run errands for her. She was on a number of medications and was getting to the point where she could not remember what she had taken or when. She had no appetite when she ate alone, so she hardly cooked at all. When her son did not take her out or bring something in, she ate cereal or sandwiches.

When I first saw her, she was malnourished because of her inadequate diet. She was overdrugged from conflicting prescriptions from various physicians and over-the-counter drugs she had chosen for herself. She would get lost if she wandered out of the house. She left doors unlocked and was an easy target for intruders. But in spite of all this she would not consider living anywhere else, while making more and more demands on her neighbors and her son. The son desperately needed a vacation. He wanted to make a long deferred trip to visit other members of the family and to get out from under the pressures. But he felt imprisoned by the care of his mother. What options were open to them?

Change challenges our adaptive capacity. The Chinese characters for "crisis" mean "dangerous opportunity." The Greek word from which we derive our word "crisis" has the connotation of a judgment. Change gives us opportunity to clarify our values, sort out our needs from our wants, and show who we are. It puts our competence and strength to a test. The response we make to a crisis is the verdict with which we have to live.

Seeing Life as Change

Our concern about our living arrangements is precipitated by change. The decision to make new arrangements involves us in further change. Sometimes we wish that things would stand still so we did not have to deal with change.

But change is not something that happens only in our later years. Change is and has been a constant and inescapable fact all through the life span. To live is to change. We confront change at every period in our lives, although there may be some ages at which change is most noticeable and some periods of history when change seems to occur more rapidly and more dramatically than others. The Greek philosopher Heraclitus came to believe that change was the basic fact of existence. He noted that no one can ever step twice in the same river. We live in a world which is in process. Often we find ourselves in a turbulent environment. Ecclesiastes, too, reminds us how things pass away and change: "For everything there is a season, and a time for every matter under heaven" (Eccles. 3:1).

1. Growth and Aging

Change comes about with the biological process of growth and aging. Children live with rapidly changing bodies that grow in capacity and open them to changing expectations. This process slows down when we come to adulthood but does not come to a halt. Actually, the aging process begins at birth, although the changes caused by aging become most noticeable in the later years in slower reflexes, diminished sensory acuity, and a slowing of convalescence from illness or injury. Our perceptions of our own bodies hardly ever keep up with the actual changes that have taken place. When we go back to our fiftieth class reunion, we wonder why our classmates have changed so much when, in our own eyes, we have hardly changed at all. Gradual change may pass unnoticed. It is sudden or rapid change that arrests our attention and demands extraordinary effort.

2. Time Marching On

Change is precipitated also by historical events. Depressions, wars, droughts, and the development of new technologies confront us with the demand to adjust our way of living. Gasoline engines made horse travel obsolete and made us dependent upon automobiles and imported oil. The development of industry lured people off farms into cities. Those of us who are past 65 were born in the time of World War I; we were children in the ferment and dislocation of the Roaring Twenties; we struggled through the Great Depression of the thirties; we experienced the adjustments of World War II; we lived to see our young people at home rebel against the Establishment and the Vietnam War. Those who were sent overseas and returned faced traumas which marked them for life.

Usually these historical changes are accompanied by changes in values, manners, and morals. These historical changes have their greatest impact upon us in adolescence and young adulthood, when we are most vulnerable to peer pressure. So as the styles, values, and manners of the most malleable age group change, rifts often separate them from the age groups less affected by peer pressure. Unless we maintain an open mind and find our security within, we may become bewildered, frightened, and angry.

3. Incidents and Accidents

Then there are those particular things that happen to us individually, such as a serious accident or illness, an opportunity we did not expect, meeting someone who changes our outlook and our life, the death of someone dear to us or upon whom we depend. The way we respond to these changes varies infinitely, for each of us is unique.

So those of us in our later maturity not only are adjusting to the biological changes brought on by aging but also to cultural and social upheavals being wrought by both technological developments and historical movements.

Attitudes Toward Change

The way we look at change makes a tremendous difference in our capacity to live with it. There are at least four ways to meet and respond to change.

1. Welcome Change

There are times when change is welcomed. There are even times when change is sought. As children we eagerly measured our growth because it enabled us to do more of the things we wanted to do and because others complimented us on it. We look forward to getting old enough to go to school, old enough to get our driver's license, old enough to vote, old enough to make our own decisions. Change then promised freedom and possibility and excitement. Change was met with hope and countered with high spirits and overflowing energy.

Children and youth deliberately look for new experience. They court adventure. They need to test their capacities and their competence against challenge. The buffeting that comes when they are up against hard tasks or face danger enriches their store of sensory memories and establishes what they are capable of doing. Persons deprived of challenge and of strong sensation may grow up mentally lazy and emotionally flabby.

Change and transformation are parts of the creative process. That which never changes is dead. When we are dissatisfied or discontent, we hope for change for the better, and we try to bring it about. The apostle Paul writes: "We know that the whole creation has been groaning in travail together until now; and not only the creation, but we ourselves, who have the first fruits of the Spirit, groan inwardly as we wait for adoption as sons, the redemption of our bodies. For in this hope we were saved" (Rom. 8:22-24). We may become creative agents of change, anticipating and guiding it, rather than passive victims of change.

2. Fear of Change

But we may get to a point in our later years where we dread change and long for stability. In fact, some persons seem to begin early in life to resent and resist change.

Recoil against change may root in satisfaction with things as they are. It is easy to become complacent when we are comfortable. So we are reluctant to give up what we see as a good thing. Any notion that things can never remain quite the same is pushed out of our minds. When change comes or is forced upon us, we resent it as an interruption of a satisfying way of life.

This is understandable, particularly in later life. Our roots in our present location may be deep. The house we live in may be furnished with mementos of great experiences we have had and be filled with precious memories. We may feel comfortable with the people we have come to know and depend on: the familiar postal worker, the grocer on the corner, the dentist, and the physician. The church we have attended for years is just down the block. We have friends all around us.

Or again, barriers to making change may be found in a basic insecurity and lack of self-confidence rooted in previous failures in dealing with change. If we have had little experience in making decisions in response to change, we are not likely to be comfortable with it.

Furthermore, change takes energy and time. When we are older, the fear of change may stem from diminished energy, whether we have grown soft from lack of exercise or weak from disease. Making decisions is hard work.

Finally, change in later maturity may seem to offer only that which is worse than what we have had, contrary to the younger years when change was for the better. No matter what we decide, there is an element of risk and uncertainty about the outcome. Not to move may face us with unknown dangers, but the benefits of moving may be even less sure, and it is hard to visualize the possible advantages. We cringe and are paralyzed by our fear.

3. Denial

Because of fear of the unknown and the stress of making adjustments, our response to changes may be a temptation to shut our eyes, pretending that changes are not happening and that we will be all right as we were before. Or we may tell ourselves that things will work out if we have a little more patience. So we make no decision, and things are allowed to drift. For example, we all know that some day we will die, but we put off making a will. We postpone thinking about our funeral or where we will be buried. We may never discuss with our spouses, children or friends what we might like for ourselves. Moving in the later years may be seen as a painful reminder that life is growing short, rather than a challenge to clarify what it is we really want.

4. Panic

Another kind of response is to act too precipitously after the death of a spouse or some other major experience. In the first flush of retirement, the period of mourning following bereavement, the recuperation from a serious illness—these are not good times to make major decisions about moving. A decision and a move made in panic is not likely to be best.

Panic sometimes takes the form of paralysis. We may just give up and surrender our lives to fate.

If we can anticipate that we are likely to need to move, it is best to make the move before the emergency arises and we are forced to make it precipitously. However, it is difficult to foresee when a move will be necessary. Many of the residents of the retirement community I served said, "The only mistake I made was not to come here five years sooner, when I could have enjoyed it more." In any case we might have some contingency plans in mind as possible responses to changes we might encounter in the future.

Christian Faith and Change

When we think of life planning in terms of our Christian responsibility, we find ourselves steering a course between two poles of thought. On one hand we have the teaching of Jesus as reported in Matthew 6:25-34 in which we are exhorted, "Do not be anxious about your life, what you shall eat or what you shall drink, nor about your body, what you shall put on. . . . Let the day's own trouble be sufficient for the day." Some have taken this as a diatribe against planning and against trying to make provision for the future. "Don't worry," they say. "If we have faith, God will take care of us."

As we interpret this scripture passage we must remember that the situation in the first century, when this was written, was quite different from what it is today. For one thing, there was a strong belief that the end of the world was very near, when God would wind up his creating, all accounts would be settled, and the Kingdom of God would be established everywhere. Therefore there was no sense in planning for the years ahead. That seems to be back of the report that the disciples in Jerusalem sold all they had and gave all into a common treasury to be used up.

For another thing life was short and not many persons lived out their allotted three score and ten. It is estimated that the life expectancy of a person at birth was less than 30 years because of the high infant mortality, the high risk associated with childbirth, and the prevalence of epidemic diseases as well as accidents. In the face of such a situation it makes more sense to focus on getting the most out of each day.

Finally, at that time whatever social security one had was dependent on one's family relationships. The extended family was expected to care for the sick, the widowed, the orphaned, and the aged. Those who for any reason were separated from a family were in bad straits. They might end up as beggars on the streets or as slaves.

The passage quoted above encourages us not to overvalue a security based on the amassing of many possessions or upon power and status, but to put our trust in doing God's will. It underscores an attitude of openness to the future. Fullness of life is to be found in observing the two great commandments—in loving the Lord our God with our whole beings and our neighbors as ourselves. Our life is to be a song of praise to God. We are to be more concerned with human relations than with material things.

So we are given the parables of Lazarus and the rich man, the rich fool and the big barn, and the rich younger ruler, none of whose wealth did them any good because they had overlooked the primary values. The promise is that for those who love God all things will work for good, so even though we walk through the valley shadowed by death, we will fear no evil.

The other pole of thought is that of the stewardship of our capacities and our possessions. We are to take responsibility for our own lives, dedicating them to the glory of God so that in union with him we may have our lives fulfilled and enriched. Here we are given the parables of the talents and of the wise and foolish virgins.

If we love God, we will love what he loves and take care of what he has created. This includes us. We are valuable because God values us. Our bodies are the temples of God's Spirit, instruments for the working out of his purposes, and are therefore to be kept in the best possible condition. God loves all persons, and therefore our neighbors are to be cherished as infinitely valuable. God loves all that he has created and therefore the things of the physical world are to be treated with respect.

The love of God and of neighbor requires the full use of our intelligence. We have a moral obligation to be aware of the possible consequences of our actions as far as we are able. As co-creators with God we must attempt to discern his blue-prints for the creation and for our lives and make this our plan for the future. In assuming this responsibility we act in faith and leave the outcome in the hands of God.

We live in a changing world, and we too change as we live through the years. Instead of letting nature take its course or counting on tradition to carry us through, we take charge of our lives and give some thought to the future. We plan our lives, not just when young, but at various turning points along the way. This means trying to face, to comprehend, and to foresee changes. It means constant clarification of our values, examination of possibilities, and the making of choices. It means taking our marching orders daily from the God whom we serve as he creates his world. It means taking the risk of going forth on a pilgrimage, looking for "the city which has foundations" (Heb. 11:10). It means provisioning ourselves for the journey in anticipation of future needs and schooling ourselves to cope with challenges we may meet.

2

Coping
with
Change

To live is to experience change and
to respond to the demand for change.
To live fully requires that we cope successfully with change
when it occurs and find appropriate ways of meeting our
needs in new circumstances. Within the context of a caring
community, with the help of friends and family, we can
cope. However, we know that the process of coping represents
a challenge.

How We Experience Change

The way we cope with change depends in part upon how
we experience change and what it means to us. Change can
be experienced as both negative and positive.

1. Negative Meanings

Coping with change entails the output of additional energy.
Consider the work involved in moving from one place to

another. Time and energy are required in selecting and deciding on a new place, changing addresses, and establishing connections with new stores, banks, utilities, and social services. It takes time to find new physicians and dentists. Sorting and packing, unpacking and arranging are hard work. As we grow older, we tend to move more slowly, and we have less energy to spend. It takes us longer to recover from strain. So *change may be experienced as fatigue*, and in later maturity fatigue is usually a greater factor than in our younger years, particularly if we have health problems or have allowed ourselves to become flabby from lack of exercise.

Coping with change means that we sustain some losses. Moving to a new location means the loss of the familiar surroundings in which we have learned to find our way almost with our eyes shut. It may mean the loss of visits with friends, the surrender of membership in a church where ties are strong. It may mean leaving behind or discarding articles of furniture and mementos which have sentimental value. For many of us our personal identities have become bound to place and property. So *change may be experienced as grief*. If change comes too thick and fast, we may find that we have taken on an overload of grief almost beyond what we can bear. For many of us later maturity brings many losses which add up and compound the grief we experience in moving.

Coping with change means making decisions between various options. This means we involve ourselves in risking the unknown. Every time we move, we have to make decisions about what to take or leave, and so, we run the risk of making a mistake. Sometimes we must choose between mutually exclusive goods in which we have to give up one in order to have the other, such as sacrificing independence for the sake of security or companionship. Change pushes us into uncertainty and the unfamiliar. So *change may be experienced as anxiety*, particularly if we have experienced failures in past ventures.

Coping with change may cause us to make choices that

conflict with our ideals or that incur the disapproval of others. Grown children often feel guilty about having an elderly mother admitted to a nursing home. The family may feel ashamed of having to accept Medicaid or Supplemental Security Income. We may feel some shame at not having managed our lives in such a way that we could have avoided the problems we now face. So *change may be experienced as shame or guilt.* These things represent the negative side of change.

2. Positive Meanings

The positive aspect of change is that it may lift us out of our rut, stimulate our minds, cause us to become more active and so enlarge our capacities and open new doors for fulfillment. The wearing out of a comfortable and familiar dress or hat or suit of clothes may catapult us into getting a new wardrobe that adds to the positive image of ourselves and earns us compliments. Moving may introduce us to new friends who reconfirm us in our worth and attractiveness. It may provide us opportunity to view new scenes and to learn new skills or gain new knowledge.

The negative aspect of change therefore may be balanced or even cancelled out by a feeling of relief at having overcome obstacles or at leaving behind some of the problems that bothered us. We may have a heightened sense of our own competence and capacity to cope with life. We may be exhilarated by the new we are experiencing. So *change can be experienced as the stirring up of life!*

Just as the eagle is said to push her eaglets out of the nest when they get too big to stay there and they are forced to spread their wings and learn to soar in order to survive, so life keeps pushing us to be more than we have been so far. *Change may be experienced as new beginnings, new opportunity.*

Understanding Stress

The problem of coping with change often is discussed under the heading of managing stress. Stress is experienced any time our equilibrium is upset or our routines are interrupted and we have to act in extraordinary ways to respond to these changes. This is particularly true when the change threatens to put us in peril.

Negatively, stress may be felt in such symptoms as loss of appetite, restlessness, sleep disturbance, tension, irritability, jumpiness, or headaches. We may be aware of dryness in the throat or the pounding of our heart. We may feel butterflies in our stomach.

Positively, stress may be felt as excitement, alertness, resolve, and boundless energy. The bodily changes that underlie these symptoms are nature's way of insuring survival. Stress prepares us for flight or fight. Adrenalin is poured into the system; the heart beats faster and delivers more blood to the muscles; the blood clots more quickly if we are wounded; the mind becomes more alert. We can run faster, jump higher, work longer, and endure more when under stress. Athletes depend upon "getting up" for a contest. Some stress is good. Sudden or overwhelming stress may cause mindless panic or make us unable to function at all.

Too much stress or stress endured too long can cause illness. It is one thing to cope with an immediate and identifiable danger which passes. It is another thing to live for weeks in the presence of danger, especially if the danger is vaguely lurking, unnamed and unknown.

Stress can be connected with changes which are on the surface completely benign and joyous. Suppose, for example, that we have inherited an estate and a large sum of money which can be claimed only if we move to Hawaii within the next six months. As exciting as this might be, the changes this threatens would put us under stress.

Two University of Washington Medical School psychiatrists, T. H. Holmes and R. H. Rahe, have developed a stress scale which has been widely circulated. On this scale events have been accorded a stress value. The list on p. 32 is based on the Holmes-Rahe research, as revised by Dr. Keith Sehnert. M.D., in *Stress/Unstress* (Augsburg, 1981).

Obviously this list is a relative weighing of the amount of stress each of these events causes, since they may have different meanings to different people in varieties of situations. But it is important to note, (1), that many different kinds of changes cause stress, and (2), when a number of these occur all at once, the stress level can get very high. In fact, the physicians who developed this scale in the course of research predicted that whenever the stress level went over 200, persons would run the risk of incurring illness. This was found to be true in their study.

The amount of stress experienced from an event depends upon expectancy and perception, both of which are rooted in prior experience. Suppose, for example, that you are walking through the woods in a mountain resort. Suddenly a large animal looms ahead. You see it as a bear because you have been told there are bears in this area. Immediately your heart begins to pound, you catch your breath and begin to breathe more rapidly. Your body is getting ready for you to run or climb. Stress here comes from a perceived danger.

Stress can also be experienced from a feared or anticipated danger. Suppose that before going on your walk you were warned that bears have been seen and that you should be careful because they are dangerous. Probably you would be under stress from the beginning, and you would be jumpy.

If, by way of contrast, you know a lot about bears and know that it is unlikely there are any in the area and that if there are, they are timid and will likely run away, you will not be so distressed by what you see. If upon a closer look the animal turns out to be a St. Bernard dog belonging to a friend, immediately you will relax. Understanding stress contributes to our ability to deal with it.

LIFE EVENT	STRESS VALUE
Death of spouse	100
Divorce	73
Marital separation	65
Jail term	63
Death of close family member	63
Personal injury or illness	53
Marriage	50
Fired at work	47
Marital reconciliation	45
Retirement	45
Change in health of family member	44
Pregnancy	40
Sex difficulties	39
Gain of new family member	39
Business readjustment	39
Change in financial state	38
Death of close friend	37
Change to a different line of work	36
Change in number of arguments with spouse	35
Mortgage over $40,000	31
Foreclosure of mortgage or loan	30
Son or daughter leaving home	29
Change in responsibilities at work	29
Trouble with in-laws	29
Outstanding personal achievement	28
Spouse begins or stops work	26
Begin or end school	26
Change in living conditions	25
Revision of personal habits	24
Trouble with the boss	23
Change in work hours or conditions	20
Change in residence	20
Change in schools	20
Change in recreation	19
Change in church activity	19
Change in social activities	19
Mortgage or loan of less than $40,000	17
Change in number of family get-togethers	15
Change in sleeping habits	15
Change in eating habits	15

Handling Stress

What can we do about stress? How can we cope better with changes when they come? Here is a list of things that various persons have found helpful:

1. Face the Reality of the Situation

Whether it is an illness that requires treatment, a physical disability that calls for adjustment in life-style, a loss that has robbed you of something valued highly, or financial need, do not try to deny it, sweep it under the rug, or put it out of mind. Except for emergency treatment given on the advice of a physician, do not take refuge in alcohol or drugs to blunt either the sharpness of your perception or your feelings about the situation. Remember that the road to the life abundant leads through challenge. Closing your eyes to change will not make it go away. If the situation is uncomfortable but still tolerable, you may have time to deal with it constructively. If you wait until a decision can no longer be evaded, your options may be drastically reduced.

2. Avoid Too Many Decisions All at Once

Try to deal with the issues one at a time in the order of their priority. Do not make decisions about moving while working your way through the shock of bereavement. Acting too precipitously at such a time may be a way of trying to run away from the reality of the loss or from the awareness of the absence of the loved one. If you let a salesman or friends pressure you into selling and moving by telling you that if you don't act immediately the opportunity will be gone, you may overlook many things that need to be considered. This is a mistake widows often make.

One way to avoid making too many decisions at one time is to anticipate changes and to pace yourself, taking them as you can manage them. This means that many decisions will be made well in advance of the time when they have to be carried out rather than at the moment of crisis. Coaches of football or baseball teams try to visualize all the situations that could possibly arise and to work out prior decisions based on known probabilities of scoring. Thus in the heat of the game they play the percentages rather than agonizing over what to do next or being forced to make decisions which they have no time to weigh carefully.

3. Acknowledge Your Feelings

Whatever they may be—anger, anxiety, shame or fear— admit your feelings. Talk about your feelings to those close to you. Your feelings have to be taken into account as part of the data about the situation. Your tastes, your preferences, your values, and your idiosyncracies need to be considered. Even if you are not able to have what you want and you have to settle for less than you had hoped for, at least you will have thought about your feelings. In the process of dealing with your feelings you may be able to correct your perceptions of the situation in such a way that your feelings will change.

4. Remind Yourself That You Can Cope

Look in the mirror, if you like, and tell yourself you can cope. You have faced many changes and hardships before and have come through them. Many other persons besides you have had to go through similar or worse circumstances, and they survived. Remember that you will not be the only one working on the problem. Try to focus on how things will be better when you get through your ordeal. Remind yourself that whatever the nature of your problem, this too will pass and there will be better days when the sun will shine and the flowers will bloom.

5. Take Time Out for Relaxation

Pursue a hobby or engage in recreation. Go on a picnic. Set aside time for meditation and prayer. Spend time visiting with persons you love and enjoy, who support you and confirm you in your worth as a person.

Relaxation exercises have been found to be helpful. For example, sit comfortably in a chair which fits you with both feet on the floor. Put your hands in your lap. Close your eyes. Deliberately relax each muscle of the body. Begin with the toes. Tighten then release. Move up to the muscles of the legs, then the thighs, the torso, shoulders, and neck. Relax the muscles of your face and forehead. Now breathe deeply four or five times slowly. Then while breathing naturally and regularly, count "one" under your breath each time you exhale.

A variation of this is to lie on the floor or on a firm bed. Do the relaxation exercise. Then when you breathe focus first on breathing with your abdomen. Then breathe by expanding your chest. Alternate breathing from the diaphragm and the chest. Then breathe naturally while counting.

Meditate on a favorite passage of Scripture, such as Psalm 23. Repeat it over and over again, visualizing the images it calls up. Imagine yourself beside the still waters or lying on the grass in green pastures or walking calmly through the valley of death.

Take time to recall the good moments of life, when you felt most good about yourself, when you were most happy. Contemplate an object of beauty such as a flower. Look at it. Study it. Savor it.

Relaxation and a confident mind-set have been found effective in reducing pain and promoting healing.

6. Exercise Regularly

Regular exercise has proved to be particularly beneficial for those under stress. Walking, swimming, playing golf—whatever you enjoy is useful for letting off steam. Calisthenics are good too. Sometimes a strenuous activity such as cleaning the basement, washing the windows, sweeping out the garage, or scrubbing the floor helps to keep the tension at acceptable levels. Too often there is a temptation to forego exercise because of an urge to focus on the stressful situation. While emergencies might preempt routine and require immediate and sustained attention for a time, it is useful to take time out to catch your breath and get some perspective. Maintaining health is important in arming oneself to deal with the pressures of coping with problems.

7. Seek Support from Others

We are members of a community. We do not live alone. Talk your situation over with a trusted confidant or with members of your family. Get advice from a professional counselor as appropriate, such as a physician, a lawyer, a real-estate broker or a financial planner. You might do well to solicit more than one opinion.

Your pastor may be able to help you face and think through your situation. Your church may have support groups or special persons to whom you could turn. Some churches have networks of persons who have been through particular crises. A widow who knows what it is to be bereaved, a parent who has lost a child, a person who has undergone surgery or radiation therapy for cancer, an alcoholic who has learned not to drink—these persons are often better able to help persons in similar situations. Some churches have small transition groups of persons who are going through a similar crisis at the same time, such as preparing for retirement.

8. Clarify What You Really Need

Try to distinguish between your basic needs and your wants. Much of the pressure we face comes from overblown expectations and fear of having to do without some of the things we have come to believe are important but really are not. Henry David Thoreau remarked that most of us go through life pushing big red barns before us. So simplify your life as much as possible. Sort out those things you surround yourself with and carry around that needlessly slow you down and sap your energy without contributing anything to your well-being. The Japanese have had to learn how to live within limited space and in an environment that yields benefits reluctantly. So they will remove almost everything from a room except for one precious and lovely object. They have learned to enjoy serving simple food on a lovely plate carefully arranged. They have made an art out of preparing and pouring tea.

9. Give Yourself Time

Be patient with yourself in working through the changes you are making. As we grow older, it takes longer to recover from illness, injury, or fatigue. It takes time to work through grief over loss and to replace that which is lost with new meanings. The pain will diminish slowly, and the memory will be with you as long as you live. But it will become part of the background against which the picture of the present is made luminous. Don't expect all problems to be solved instantly or seeds to sprout and bloom overnight.

10. When Depressed—Do Something

One response to continuing stress is to become depressed. When depressed we feel low. We can't enjoy anything. We are unable to decide or to act. We lose our appetites. We may become withdrawn. In such a situation usually it is wise to consult a physician who may be able to prescribe antidepressant drugs to help us over the crisis. Also usually it helps if we can make ourselves do something even if we don't feel like it, such as going for a walk, cleaning the cupboard, or scrubbing the floor. Physical activity is especially helpful in working through our despair. In some cases punching a pillow or screaming might help.

11. Cultivate a Sense of Humor

Humor is a way of putting things in perspective and appreciating the irony or the ludicrousness of many situations. Make a scrapbook of cartoons or jokes that reflect your situation. Go to see a funny movie or play, or watch a TV comedy show.

12. Remember God Is in This with You

This is God's world, and he is working to resolve the difficulty. His will is unity, peace, justice, and love. His Spirit is moving on the face of the deep to bring order out of the chaos. The forces of life are carrying you along in the direction of his purpose. Trust in God, and put some of the burden on him.

Turn to Psalm 46:

> God is our refuge and strength,
> a very present help in trouble.
> Therefore we will not fear
> though the earth should change,
> though the mountains shake
> in the heart of the sea;
> though its waters roar and foam,
> though the mountains tremble

with its tumult.

. . . . .

The Lord of hosts is with us;
The God of Jacob is our refuge.

Moving in Faith

Dr. J. Cotter Herschberg, chief of professional services and Distinguished Professor of Psychiatry at the Menninger Foundation in Topeka, Kansas, told a seminar for clergy and physicians:

> The aging process can be slowed down by the individual's belief in his continued ability to cope, by his activity in reality, and by a relevant faith.

He went on to say:

> By concentrating on the present use of faith, the older person can avoid one of the pitfalls of growing old: namely, idealizing the past. If the elderly person is helped to think about faith as it is being experienced, felt, and used today—not as it was idealized in the glorious past of the sunny summer afternoons of 1910—then the individual is helped out of the past and into the meaningfulness of his faith in the present.

Religion can be used for relevance, not for reminiscences, but to face and deal with the present problems, to cope with today's dilemmas and today's difficulties.

In an address given before a conference of seminary professors, Reuel Howe emphasized that the movement toward life demands that we draw upon our faith to accept risk. To recoil in fear from the challenges of living is to move toward death. There is no ultimate security or complete safety in this existence. We can live only this day that is given us when it comes. To choose life we must face uncertainty, endure the strain of adjusting to change, and take the risks of acting on our decisions. We begin to die when we withdraw into ourselves, retreat from making decisions, avoid struggle, and refuse to change.

This truth can be put into the form of a diagram like this:

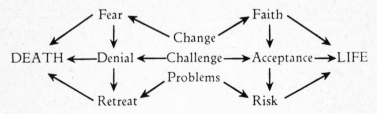

The Bible contains many stories of persons who moved from one place to another, sustained by faith and impelled by hope. The images of life as nomadic wandering, as pilgrimage, and as living through exile abound, balanced by stories of recovery, return, and deliverance from slavery. Sometimes the Hebrew patriarchs went out looking for a better place. Sometimes they were driven out by events beyond their control. Sometimes they were carried away as captives.

Abram left Haran as his father before him had quit Ur of the Chaldees, looking and trusting in God's promise to make him the founder of a great nation. His journey was long and hard.

Lot, being forewarned of the doom of Sodom and Gomorrah, where his family had lived happily for a long time, fled to the hills and was saved. But Lot's wife, unable to free herself from bondage to the past, kept looking back. So she was turned into a pillar of salt, a monument to death.

David gave up his life as a shepherd to become attendant to a king. Then he had to flee for his life from the court, wandering as a refugee in the desert before becoming king himself.

The writer of the letter to the Hebrews recounts the saga of these heroes of the faith and then observes:

> They all died in faith, not having received what was promised but having seen it and greeted it from afar,

and having acknowledged that they were strangers and exiles on the earth. For people who speak thus make it clear they are seeking a homeland. If they had been thinking of that land from which they had gone out, they would have had opportunity to return. But as it is they desire a better country, that is, a heavenly one. Therefore, God is not ashamed to be called their God, for he has prepared for them a city (Heb. 11:13-16).

God's call comes in strange ways. It may be heard in the death of persons we loved and counted on. It may come through divorce, failure, closed doors, and unexpected opportunities. When it comes, it may be telling us to go forth, to leave the settled hearth and to go out into the desert. Sooner or later most of us live part of our lives as refugees, although those of us who live here in North America can have little appreciation of what being a refugee means to millions of displaced persons around the world.

So listen to God's promise which comes with his call. Go out trusting in his covenant to be with you in loneliness, to sustain you when you are hard pressed and to give you strength to overcome when you need it. Read Psalm 139 and Romans 8:28-39. No matter where you go you will never be separated from his love.

3

Choosing Your Future

As we get older, many of us become anxious about our future and worry constantly about what will happen to us. Many of our adult children are deeply concerned about the increasing vulnerability of their aging parents. The kinds of problems that emerge with age are new to us and to them. We are unfamiliar with the resources available to us in the community and do not know how to go about finding them. We wonder to whom we may turn for advice and counsel. What we would like to do or what we feel we ought to do may not be either possible or feasible. So anxiety and concern are aggravated by lack of knowledge, confusion about the best path to take, and possibly guilt about not being able to do what we feel is right.

However, we can make some choices about our future, even though those choices may not be what we would like best. We do not need to let the future merely happen to us like an avalanche hurtling down a mountain. We always have a measure of freedom within which we can decide what we will do, what kind of person we will be, and how we will relate to others.

Responses That Do Not Help

One response to change is to do nothing. However, not to make a decision is, in effect, a decision, which has consequences for us. Doing nothing and putting off any effort to decide may be more comfortable for a while, but sooner or later the problem will catch up with us, and by that time it may be too late to make a better choice. We can put a problem out of mind and ignore an obvious need in the hope that it will go away or that something will turn up to solve it. Usually the decision not to decide is a decision to overlook opportunities. It is a choice of death rather than life.

Dora, a brilliant and charming woman who has had a successful career, has been a community leader, and has been a gracious, understanding, and supportive wife and mother, suffered a series of small strokes that gradually impaired her memory and her ability to function. This happened in her early seventies. The knowledge of what was happening to her terrified her at first and then depressed her as she despaired of recovery and worried about being a burden. But in keeping with a lifelong pattern of problem solving, she resolved to keep the burdensomeness of her illness for others to a minimum by being as responsible for herself and as cooperative as she could. She drew upon the resources of her faith and support of her family and friends to face down the fear. The courage with which she faced her waning strength was an inspiration to her family and friends. She and her husband faced the issue posed by organic brain deterioration and made plans for a series of steps they could take as her condition grew worse.

Another response is to recognize that things have changed but to vow that you will "tough it out" come what may, trusting yourself to fate. You will resist change to the last ditch. This response is usually coupled with a refusal to accept any counsel or trust any proposal for adjusting to the change. Often I have heard people say, "I am going to stay right here until I am carried out. I will make it somehow."

In almost any large city one may see a so-called "bag woman" who keeps all her possessions in a shopping bag, rummages in garbage cans for food and clothes, and sleeps in doorways or under bridges if she no longer has a decaying hovel of her own. Social workers and social agencies are baffled by the refusal of such persons to accept any help or cooperate with any long-term solution to their problems.

Glenda and Marie, friends, are both in their eighties. Glenda adamantly refuses to leave her home or get rid of the furniture which crams her space. She scorns hospitals, retirement homes, nursing homes. She has made no effort to find out what resources the community offers. Marie has already moved to a smaller apartment and has disposed of most of her accumulation of things. She is considering a move to a retirement home. She is familiar with nursing homes and social services. Neither understands the other's attitudes.

A third kind of unhelpful response is to panic and to act precipitously before checking out all the options and making a considered decision based upon a careful study of the situation. A sudden and unanticipated illness or accident, the loss of a spouse, or some natural catastrophe may induce panic and the urge to flee. Sometimes rumors of rezoning or new freeways or urban renewal or coming crime waves cause persons to panic. Unscrupulous operators may spread rumors in order to take advantage of panic selling.

A fourth unhelpful response is to react to social pressures or to the advice of well-meaning friends and relatives who may be all too willing to tell you what you ought to do. Widows indicate that they receive all sorts of advice and pressure from others urging them to sell their homes and move immediately. Or they are told that they should go and live with some of their relatives. This social pressure compounds the tendency to act too quickly.

Our adult children may feel under pressure from neighbors or kin either to have us move in with them or to move in with us, if the child is single. Anything else is interpreted by others as rejection or as "putting away" the parent. So friends and children may pressure us to do what we may not be ready to do. These pressures may close our eyes to new and creative possibilities for the later years and stand in the way of satisfying relationships between the elderly parent and the adult child.

A fifth unhelpful response is to slam the door on the future by making others promise never to do something or by binding oneself against doing something. James told his daughter, "Never put me in a nursing home!" When eventually nursing care was needed that she was unable to provide, she was torn by feelings of guilt and delayed the move, to the detriment of all. Ralph expressed interest in moving into a well-managed church-sponsored retirement home after his wife died. The other members of the family insisted they would not "put one of their own into that place" without ever checking it out—until it became too late.

Finally, except in times of emergencies when we are definitely incompetent to decide because of extreme illness, *it is not helpful for others to take the decision out of our hands and to make the choice for us.* Sometimes our children assume that because their parents are along in years they must be senile and therefore have to be treated as children. This forces us into the role of the child or of the helpless patient. We may resent such action and may feel it is a blow to our self-esteem and ego strength.

Sometimes, by refusing to act, we older people may consciously or unconsciously try to trap our children into making the decision for us. Then we can say, "You put me away," or "You closed your door on me," thus using guilt to exact favors from them.

The question for the older person of when to surrender responsibility and control over their lives to others or, for a caretaker, when to assume that responsibility without the permission of the older person is not an easy one. It can only be addressed in dialogue between the parties concerned, as long as dialogue is possible. Even if the time comes when an adult child or other person believes there is no other course to take but to act on behalf of the older person, as far as possible this should be fully explained to the older person, if he or she is conscious. Usually, if there is a good working relationship between us and our adult children or some other caretaker, this question can be resolved by mutual agreement.

If we are in possession of our mental faculties and able to consider the consequences of any decisions made, we want others to respect our right to remain in charge of our own life and to choose how and where we will live. Our care-takers, however, also have a right to resist manipulation or exploitation and to declare their own needs. The principle of the relationship between us older persons and our caretakers has to be based on the commitment to love the neighbor as the self. This implies mutuality and self-regard rather than the sacrifice of one to the other. In the past for too many years the youngest daughters were expected to ignore their own needs and devote their lives to care for an aged parent who drained them of selfhood and vitality.

Ground Rules for Problem Solving

After this quick review of responses that are not helpful we look at some general principles that apply to all kinds of problem situations. In some cases these are the opposite of the responses that are not helpful.

1. *All parties involved in the living arrangements of an older person should participate in the decision-making process.* Since the older persons are the ones most deeply involved and most affected by the decisions, generally they should have the final say in what is done. However, adult children, grand-children, nieces and nephews, even brothers and sisters may be involved in terms of visitation, running errands, providing some services, and contributing to the cost. So they need to have some say about the final arrangements to the extent that

their lives are being affected. The decision-making process then is one of negotiation and balancing of needs and values.

For example, after Mrs. Benedict's husband died, she did not want to live alone. In her panic she assumed she would live with her grown children, spending a period of time visiting with each of them. During the first year the children went along with this arrangement, desiring to support her in her grief. But none of them was in a position to have her move in permanently, and long visits were not satisfactory to Mrs. Benedict. She could not put down roots in any community to replace those she had torn up, and she could not have a place of her own to entertain friends or do what she wanted. So the children had to tell her graciously but firmly that she needed to find an apartment of her own, that they could not keep her permanently. Finally a joint decision was made for her to live in an apartment near one of her daughters and one of her sons. Unfortunately Mrs. Benedict and her husband had not thought through what they would do when either of them died. The extent of her dependence and her quick assumption that she could live with one of her children had come as a surprise to them all, for Mrs. Benedict had always said she did not want to be the burden to her children that her mother had been to her.

2. *Deal openly with feelings and values*, for these are two important considerations in the decision-making process. Chief among these are feelings about independence and privacy on one side and dependence and need for companionship on the other. The kind of long-term relationships we have had with other members of our family must be considered in any decision to live with or near them. When relationships have always been distant or broken, hostile and conflicted, living together may be disastrous. If they have been close, loving, cooperative, mutually supportive, they may be rewarding. Cultural conditioning having to do with religion, tastes in food, or ethnic festivals may affect a person's ability to enjoy living cut off from a setting where these are found.

3. *Except in real emergencies avoid making hasty deci-*

sions, and try not to make too many decisions all at once. Try rather to anticipate eventualities and develop some contingency plans for various eventualities.

As we discussed in Chapter 2, widows quite frequently move too quickly after the death of their husbands. Sometimes they do not want to face the familiar things that bring back memories of their loved ones. Sometimes they are afraid to be alone. Sometimes they accede to well-meaning friends who too readily tell them to move away. So they move and then find it was a mistake.

Sometimes couples decide to move to a resort community in a completely different part of the country, often far from support facilities such as physicians, hospitals, stores, and cultural amenities. The wife is left alone in a new and strange community. She may be isolated by distance and in some cases not even able to drive a car, which is the only means of transportation. The couple did not think far enough ahead and consider the things that might happen.

4. *If at all feasible take time to visit and test out possible locations before deciding.* It is wise to become somewhat familiar with various resources and different kinds of housing in the community long before the need arises to make a change. If a move to another climate or another part of the country is contemplated, vacation time might be used to test out the situation. Sometimes it is possible to rent an apartment or motel room for a time before buying a house in a new area, and still maintain ownership of the old, in case we decide not to move. This way bridges are not burned, and we are not tied to the new by ownership of property. Several different locations may be tried out.

The Issue of Incompetence

Probably the thing most of us dread the most is "losing our minds," being unable to decide for ourselves what we will do. The probability of actually "losing our minds" is very small. Only about ten percent of the elderly experience real organic brain syndrome (organic damage which is irreversible) and only about half of that number are truly incompetent. However, what is commonly called "senility," (a term which the medical profession is increasingly eager to scrap as meaningless), and which is marked by confusion, by delusions, loss of memory, and peculiar mannerisms, may be caused many things such as malnutrition, infections, loss of sight and hearing, overuse of drugs and medications, or environmental stress. We are discovering that many of these are treatable and reversible.

However, there is always the possibility that because of accident or illness we may become unable to act on our own behalf and may be forced to depend on others to make crucial decisions for us. One way to deal with this is to make provisions beforehand for this eventuality. By making wills, by leaving written instructions, by nominating guardians, designating conservators of our estate or person, setting up trusts, or giving power of attorney, we can make it easier for those who will have to take care of us. In some cases joint bank accounts insure that someone can draw on our funds to pay our bills. However, a lawyer should be consulted before making these moves.

If we postpone all these decisions until incompetence occurs, then we will have to depend upon others to act on our behalf. Relatives may have themselves designated by the courts to act as guardians or conservators. For those of us who have no relatives or close friends, there are in most counties public guardians who can be appointed to act as conservators and guardians.

The assessment of mental competence may be made jointly by the person involved and by physicians. That is, we may initiate a request for an assessment when we feel that we are no longer competent or do not have the strength to manage our own affairs and need to have someone else take over and manage for us. We may not even need help to make such an assessment if we have come to the point where we find ourselves unable to function and we can take steps to locate a caretaker.

On the other hand, the assessment may be initiated by others who are responsible for us and yet who may not be legally able to take charge. So they may petition the courts to assess competence and to assign responsibility accordingly. In either case both the person and the estate are protected by legal safeguards.

The Issue of Indigence

Then there is the possibility of running short of resources and of having to resort to what is too frequently called "welfare" or "charity." We Americans still tend to believe that poverty represents a personal failure and moral weakness, that suffering is just recompense for past sins. Social Security is acceptable because we see clearly how we have contributed to it. Supplemental Security Income (S.S.I.), available to those whose income and assets fall below a certain level, is often felt to be unacceptable because we forget that as citizens and taxpayers we have all contributed over the years to create a community in which each person can be protected with a "floor" to their income. This is true also of Medicare (all right because we pay something for it) and Medicaid (available when we become "medically indigent," a term of approbrium meaning our income and assets make it impossible to pay all of our medical bills).

The assessment of financial need is made in consultation with financial advisors, representatives from the Social Security Administration, and in some cases from city or county departments of human services.

The point here is that either incompetence or indigence is a possibility for any one of us and needs to be considered in our planning. If it happens, it can be dealt with, although unfortunately community resources are still far too limited to meet human needs on a satisfactory level for all persons. If we are aware that it can happen to us, we may become more concerned to lend our influence to the development of community resources as a kind of insurance. Another point to be made is that as members of a human community we have a right to draw on the resources of that community according to need, as well as have a responsibility to contribute to that community according to our ability.

Steps Toward a Decision

Experience has taught us that there are some logical steps to take in the process of problem solving and decision making. Paying attention to these steps may save both time and missteps. These may be worked through formally or they may be done informally and rather intuitively. In many cases it is useful to work them out on paper so that all the elements to be considered in the decision can be kept in mind.

1. Define the Problem

A decision can be sound only to the extent the real problem has been defined and addressed. Sometimes what may seem to be the problem at first glance is not the problem at all when we look deeper into the situation. On a sheet of paper write the answers to such questions as these:

A. What has changed? Where do you hurt? What do you lack? For example, have you retired? Does this mean you are bored? at loose ends? missing the companions you worked with? income now insufficient? Would going back to work solve these problems? Or could they be solved in another way?

Or again, have you lost a spouse or life companion? Are you in shock and grief? lonely? feeling useless and unloved? Still another, is your physical capacity diminished? Does this mean you can't drive, climb stairs, lift heavy burdens, engage in recreation as you once did?

Perhaps the neighborhood has changed and deteriorated. Is it merely unsightly? Are you afraid to stay there any longer? Are there no facilities such as grocery and drug stores left?

B. How serious are these changes? Should you shrug them off, try to live with them, or respond to them?

C. Do you anticipate more or greater changes occurring in the future which will make the situation worse? Or will things remain about the same? Or get better?

2. Assess Your Resources and Liabilities

Resources and liabilities go far to determine the limits within which choices can be made as well as indicating directions in which you should move. Write these answers on another sheet.

A. What is your physical condition? mental condition? What is your present state? What is the prognosis for the future? Is your condition stable or changing? Are there things you need to be doing to maintain your health that you are not now doing? What special needs do you have?

B. What financial and monetary resources can you draw upon? Do you have pensions? Will they remain the same as long as you live? increase? decrease? What are your savings and investments? What are they likely to become in the future? Do you have insurance benefits that can be available to you as cash, or to pay catastrophic costs such as illness or fire? What public programs of assistance could you draw upon if needed? Can you anticipate gifts from others in goods, money, or services?

C. What are your personal strengths, skills, resources? What education, training, and experience can you draw on? What personality characteristics and talents do you have? What personal and spiritual strength do you possess?

D. What informal support networks can you depend on to help you? What about relatives? What about your friends? How much can you depend upon neighbors as a resource?

3. *Prioritize Your Needs*

Now, in the light of the problem to be solved and the resources you have to work with, we move to a description of what we need and what we would like. It is helpful to distinguish between *needs* which are *must-haves* and *wants* which are the *like-to-haves*. So first put down what you *must* have. Then on a separate sheet put down the things you *would like* to have.

You might respond to the following question, among others:

1. As long as I am reasonably healthy and able-bodied:
   What *must* I have in a place to live?
   > How much space? How many rooms?
   > What facilities to carry out specific activities?
   > What is the absolute limit on amount to spend each month?
   > All on one floor?
   > Will I rent or buy?
   > Storage facilities?
   > Is location important?
   > What about access to community services?
   > What about cultural amenities?

   What *would I like* but could do without if necessary?
   > How important is the landscape or the view?
   > What about the climate?
   > What about security and safety?
   > Guest rooms? entertainment facilities?
   > Privacy?
   > Whom would I like to be near?

1. If I become frail and unable to drive a car . . . ?

2. If I need protective care and a supportive environment . . . ?

3. If I need nursing care . . . ?

4. Check Out the Options Open to You

Now you can begin to look for those resources that will meet the needs which have highest priority. We will look at a number of these options in the next chapters. At this point you may want to consult persons and agencies who can supply you with more information about places to live if you need to move, and services which are available to meet special needs which are not now being met.

5. Compare the Options

On another sheet of paper compare various options for living arrangements with each other according to their fit with your priorities and wants. On the left side list your priorities. In columns to the right check off the extent to which each possible option meets the criteria you have set up for selection of a solution.

An illustration might look like this:

	Priorities	Option 1	Option 2	Option 3
must have	$300 per month top amount on housing; $250 desired amount	$275	$325	$300
would like	apartment located near shopping centers	5 blocks	2 miles out	1 block
	access to medical services	hospital clinic doctors near	doctor's office only	doctors' hospital near
	church			
	etc.			

6. Balance Alternatives

If the choice comes down to two options and you need to go deeper into an analysis of the choices you face, you might find it helpful to balance alternatives in terms of the best and worst imaginable consequences that could be anticipated in either case.

An example might look like this:

Option 1 Continue working		Option 2 Retire	
Best	Worst	Best	Worst
Enjoy income	Take pressure	Freedom to do what I want	Bored, with nothing to do
Increase value of pension	Never get to enjoy pension	Free from pressure	Run out of funds
Satisfaction of service	Possibility of being fired	Work at things I believe in	Lack stimulation to keep growing

We said earlier that every decision entails a degree of risk. Every decision involves a trade-off between values. However, when you have made your decision, although you may be tempted to look back at times and wonder what would have happened if you had decided differently, remember you can go only forward. Surely new problems will be encountered in the new place, but with God's grace you can work through them.

4

The Options for Housing: Relocating

Looking at the possibilities for moving to a new place in response to changing needs, we are reminded of those games like Parcheesi and Monopoly where one throws dice and advances according to the numbers thrown. Depending upon where one lands, there are a number of different paths that may be taken to the final goal, including detours, dead ends, and returns to square one. Until we start looking at the options for housing, we may not be aware that there are so many possibilities to choose from or that one can take different paths in getting there.

No matter which path we take, we all live in hope that we will not have to spend time in a nursing home, endure a long and lingering illness, or die slowly over a period of months. But while hoping for the best and doing all we can to avoid ill health, there is still a one-out-of-five probability that we will have to spend at least some time in a nursing home, convalescent hospital, or rehabilitation center. This does not mean that we will necessarily be there a long time, for we may be discharged to return to our own home, and it does not mean that we will certainly die there. Most people say they want to live in their own homes, where they can be independent, have privacy, and feel as though they are in control. We prize the freedom to plan our own schedules, to select what we eat, wear, and use, and to decide with whom we will associate.

When illness strikes, though, and we need expert nursing care, it is good to know that there are hospitals, health centers, and nursing homes to meet our needs. If we are aware of the kinds of needs that persons may incur, we will be more responsible in supporting the development of a community in which these needs can be met, if for no other reason than to have some insurance for ourselves. So let's consider the whole range of options before us.

The Range of Housing Options

A way of getting perspective on the number of choices you may have is to arrange the options on a continuum from independent living in a typical community to institutional care. Living independently may involve moving from a large house to a smaller one, from a detached, one-family house to a town-house or garden apartment where outside maintenance is provided for a monthly fee. Or one may prolong the capacity to live independently by adding supports such as having someone move in with you, by hiring help, or by contracting for home services. The amount of assistance given by relatives and neighbors makes a difference in where one can live.

One may choose a semi-sheltered situation which provides easy access to services and social amenities such as an apartment house or retirement hotel planned for older people, a planned retirement community or a retirement home offering congregate living plus a continuum of care in one location. Finally, if more care is needed and there are no other options, one may choose an institutional setting. (Although acute hospitals, clinics, and day-care centers are institutions, the term "in-

Figure 1. Categories of Living Arrangements

Independent living in the community	Supported living in the community	Semisheltered care retirement community	Institutional care
Live in home one owns	Others move in to share the home	Free-standing unit or cottage	Board and care home
Live in rented home	Move in with others	Apartment or hotel room	
	Hire help or use home-care services	Congregate living	Intermediate nursing care
	Day-care center	Day-hospital	Skilled nursing care
			Hospital
			Hospice

Increasing amount of protection and care by others → → → → →

stitutional care" usually refers to long-term care where the institution becomes one's home.)

The figure given on p. 59 (Figure 1) illustrates this continuum of housing options and living arrangements. As one moves from independent living in the community toward institutional care, one opts for a greater degree of safety, protection, and security, particularly with respect to health care. Costs can be expected to rise with the increase in services, whether home services or services given in an institutional setting.

Housing Is Not Enough

As we look at all these options we need to remind ourselves that housing by itself is not enough. Most of us know this intuitively, even though it is seldom stated. When we look for a place to live, we take note of the neighborhood. We want to know how it looks, who else lives there. We ask about the availability of services. We take in the general appearance and the view from the site.

There seems to be an assumption on the part of some housing developers and real estate brokers that if adequate shelter is available, all the other things will be added automatically in due time. But this is not necessarily so. Housing programs for the elderly too often overlook the importance of the supportive networks and social services which underlie a community, knit it together, and make it comfortable. The dilemma is that as services are added, costs go up. So the tendency is to provide a minimum at the lowest feasible cost and skip on the amenities.

The structure of the community can be illustrated as shown in the diagram on p. 61.

"Infrastructure" is the term often used to designate such things as roads, streets, sewers, power and gas lines, sidewalks, and fixed transportation systems such as streetcar lines. The

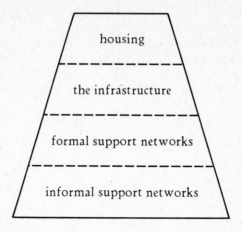

infrastructure is the physical structure that enables a modern community to function.

The "formal support networks" include such things as garbage collection, police protection, the criminal justice and penal system, medical systems and programs, school systems, stores, shopping centers, utilities, and services of all kinds.

The "informal support networks" include kinfolk, friends, neighbors, fellow club members, and members of religious bodies with whom we interact and exchange services. The quality of life in any place where we choose to live depends largely on the presence and the adequacy of these support systems that make any housing livable. So in looking for a place to live we will evaluate the things that underlie housing.

Unfortunately, very few communities have sufficient housing to meet the specific needs of all older persons in safe and pleasant neighborhoods where requisite supporting services are readily available. For many older people the problem is compounded by incomes inadequate to enable them to compete for scarce facilities. Many have to settle for less-than-desirable housing. This problem is even more severe in rural areas where it has been estimated that as many as 30% of the older people live in substandard housing and 40% to 50%

of them spend a disproportionate share of their income for housing.

With this in mind we will look in more detail at some of the main options for housing suitable to our needs.

The Old Homestead

Before talking about relocating, let us address the question of whether to move at all. Perhaps we should plan to stay where we are.

If a person retires in reasonably good health, say at age 65, he or she probably will have 10 to 15 active years to look forward to. If one's spouse is living, or if one is living with a housemate (and if not, and a person does not mind living alone) and the expense of maintaining the place is not too great, life can go on as it has in the old familiar location. In fact, it would be quite reasonable, if one is so inclined, to look forward to catching up on maintenance around the house and yard that one has not been able to get at before. During the first years of retirement many men spend time painting the house, repairing broken appliances, refinishing furniture, cleaning the yard, building in extra conveniences, or enlarging or enhancing the flower beds.

If there are neighbors or workmen who can look after the home when one is away, one may feel free to take the trips one has wanted to take, knowing that the pets will be tended and the flowers watered. If a person drives his or her own car, if children and friends come and occupy the guest rooms occasionally, and if one can keep up relationships in church and community, the old home may be the best possible place and the most satisfying.

Apartment dwellers and others who have rented rather than owned over the years may feel the same way about their familiar neighborhood. Others who have moved around a great deal following economic opportunity or career demand may not have deep roots in the community where they are living when they retire. They may plan to move back to the old home town where they do have roots and settle down there. This is a return to the familiar and the familial.

So if we like the house and the neighborhood where we now live, if we have ties to friends, relatives, and social groups, if we can take care of and maintain the place without strain on energy or income, and if we see no impending change in these conditions, we may decide to stay where we are. If we see changes coming and we can discover that there are resources in the community we can tap when we need them, we may still decide to stay put. But if changes are imminent and the resources for home care are limited, now may be the time to start looking for a new location.

One reason for selling the old homestead is that the ownership of the house may represent most of our capital assets. All our savings may be tied up in ownership, and as long as we own it, we cannot draw on our savings. Some states are experimenting with Home Equity Liquifying Plans (HELP) in which persons can continue to live in the house until they die but draw down their equity as needed. This includes such things as deferred-payment loans for property taxes, home repairs, and bills, a deferred-payment loan with or without annuity, a sale-leaseback, or sale of remainder interest. If our move is necessitated solely by the need to regain our capital, we might explore these options with our financial advisers.

A Smaller Place

If our present home or neighborhood is not satisfactory, what can we do? How about a smaller place?

When persons reach their seventies, and often before, they begin to think of housing that is less demanding for maintenance, that provides more security, is more accessible to stores, churches, and public transportation, or costs less to live in. So for some of us the first move is to a smaller house in the same community. It probably is not taxed as highly, does not cost as much to heat in the winter or cool in the summer, and is easier to clean.

Unfortunately, because of trends in real-estate development in the past several decades, the smaller houses are likely to be found in older parts of the community or in small towns. Houses built recently in the new suburbs tend to be larger, more luxurious, and equipped with more machinery to maintain. They are erected to appeal to growing families with rising incomes. This is not to say that smaller houses cannot be found. But the neighborhood and the community in which they are located need to be checked out carefully.

Apartments can usually be rented. Now there is a strong trend to converting rental units into condominiums in which one buys the apartment and then pays a monthly fee for management and services. In some cases those who rented have been faced with the announcement that they had a choice between buying and moving out.

Another option which is becoming increasingly common and popular is that of the townhouse or garden apartment. Most of these are sold as condominiums. These attract young couples without children—especially when both are career-oriented—and older people either retired or soon to retire. Most are planned with clubhouses or community centers with swimming pools and tennis courts. Common areas are owned by the association. A monthly maintenance fee pays for the care of the yard, the maintenance of the exterior of the units, and the cost of the clubhouse. Some are managed by committees of residents. Others contract with a professional management firm or hire managers.

The advantage of the apartment, townhouse, and garden apartment is that one who wants to travel can walk out, lock the door, and leave without worrying about the yard. The yard work, other than that connected with a small patio, is taken care of. Another advantage is easy access to recreational facilities and the opportunity to meet one's neighbors.

The disadvantages may be rooted in conflicts that can develop between members as they try to work out policies regarding rules and restrictions and set budgets for services. Another disadvantage has been that some developers have kept control of them for so long a time that residents have little voice in the operation. In some cases the developers have failed to provide what they promised by way of landscaping, streets, and recreational facilities. Occasionally management proves to be less than satisfactory.

More and more people are changing housing and location to fit changing needs rather than staying in one kind of domicile as long as they live. So housing is evolving to fit the phases of the life cycle. If smaller, more convenient, and more easily managed housing is available in our community, we may consider moving. As long as we stay in the community we avoid some of the trauma of breaking ties with our supportive network.

Residence in a New Community

On retirement or a few years later there may be good reason not only to move to a smaller place but to seek a different community. Those who try to go back to where they grew up may discover that the old home town has changed so much that it can never be what they remembered. They may have changed so much that they cannot be happy there again. It may lack facilities and services that are needed.

Sometimes persons who have retired experience a drop in their income and discover that the community they have been living in now costs more than they can afford. So they look for a community where taxes are lower and other costs of living are not so high. Perhaps they look for a quieter community.

Sometimes persons find the climate where they live to be intolerable and seek one more mild. In some cases children may have moved to another state. So they want to be nearer them. This assumes that the children are well-rooted and will not pull up stakes and move again soon.

In any case it is wise to check out a new community thoroughly before deciding to move there. Some use their vacations to try out a variety of settings, climates, and locations. A vacation might not be a fair test, but it does give a person a chance to become familiar with a community. It may be wise to rent for a time before selling one's home and buying in the new place. This way bridges are not burned, and one does not get locked in through ownership of property.

There are several special types of communities that we can look into. We will talk about them one by one.

The Resort Community

Around the country where there are lakes, mountains, seashore, where land is fairly cheap and plentiful, where the scenery is outstanding, resorts have been developed. Sometimes persons spend their vacations in these idyllic spots, fall in love with them and decide to move there when they retire. One may dream of owning a house on the shore of a lake with a boat moored on the back porch where fishing is good.

Such a setting may prove, at least for a time, to be just what one wants. The peace and quiet, the beauty of the surroundings, the convenience to recreation such as fishing, hiking, boating, or playing golf satisfy deeply. Space to grow a garden and flowers is appreciated.

However, these resorts, designed for tourists and vacationers, may be far from such essentials as physicians, hospitals, drugstores, or churches. They may be isolated from cultural amenities such as plays, orchestras, and even shopping centers. Groceries and services may be expensive. There may be no transportation systems other than one's own car and one may have to drive considerable distance to get anywhere.

Far too often, I am told by pastors who serve such communities, persons who move there are escaping from something in the city, such as noise, crime, crowding or racial conflict, rather than choosing an environment which has what they most deeply need. So they may be disappointed by the quality of life there. They may come to realize that there is more to life than fishing. Not infrequently a husband dies soon after the move, leaving a widow alone in a strange community with a house, a boat, and no support network.

So if we decide to move to a resort community, probably we would do well to think of this as an interim arrangement for our most active years. Then we will have another plan in mind to fall back on when conditions change.

The Planned Retirement Community

While resorts may become in effect retirement communities, usually they are not planned that way. Many communities in the so-called Sun Belt have become retirement communities because older people have moved there in numbers looking for a better climate and a cheaper place to live. This has stimulated developments in which houses are built to appeal to older owners—smaller in size, on one floor, surrounded by small lots, and emphasizing ease of maintenance. However, other aspects of community life may have been left to individual initiative and happenstance.

More recently imaginative developers have built complete communities designed especially for older persons. Central to the planning are clubhouses, recreational facilities, and sometimes walls and security guards. Land for churches and shopping centers may be set aside in the plan. A range of living accommodations all the way from free-standing houses to apartments, nursing homes, and hospitals may be planned either on or adjacent to the grounds themselves. Generally these developments are aimed at an upper-middle-class clientele, persons who have the income to move and to buy fairly expensive property and to maintain a luxurious recreational complex of golf courses, swimming pools, bowling lanes, tennis courts, and craft workshops.

These are communities focused on a life of leisure and recreation as well as freedom from many of the chores of home maintenance. Such communities usually are restricted to adults over 55 years of age, with children and young people limited to short visits. Opportunities for volunteer community service may be limited especially when the community is new and before some of the residents have grown older. Frequently they are built in an isolated area some distance from urban centers. Most are livable only if one can drive a car. Some do provide transportation and plan excursions to attend cultural and recreational events in the city.

The merits of an age-segmented community versus integrated communities can be debated according to personal preference. Usually the choice of a planned retirement community is a choice for peace, security, and order over against the excitement, surprises, disorder, and noise of children. It is a choice for noninvolvement or minimal involvement, a choice for a playful life.

Jim and Marilyn Jones moved to such a community in the Southwest when he retired from his post as chief engineer and vice-president of a large construction company. After moving they joined one of the private clubs. Jim plays golf three days a week, is active in a service club, and is a member of a bowling team. Marilyn serves as a volunteer in the library. They attend one of the churches in the community. They bicycle almost daily. Marilyn does not drive but can use the electric golf cart to go to the market, church, and the homes of her friends, many of whom they knew from their former residence.

To summarize, planned retirement communities are age segregated. They provide an integration of housing and services, especially recreational facilities, in a noninstitutional environment. They tend to be composed of older people who are both active and affluent when they move in.

If we are not too deeply involved where we are and find it more difficult to make friends, if we enjoy active recreational activities such as golf, bowling, swimming, and bicycling, if we are able bodied and mobile, if we drive and do not mind the age segregation and isolation, if we like the geographical setting, and if we happen to have previous friends or acquaintances there, we might choose to move to a planned retirement community.

One thing to keep in mind is that communities of any kind, like persons, grow, change, age and sometimes die. As communities become older, they tend to contain a wider range of ages and a greater variety of facilities to meet a spectrum of human needs. A new suburb which attracts mainly young families changes when children grow up; parents are left in an empty nest and may even bring their older parents to live with them. Eventually many of the residents retire. Other older people move in to be near their children. Eventually even the infrastructure ages, becomes obsolete and has to be replaced. A new planned retirement community may be settled primarily by couples in their sixties. But within a few years there will be widows, widowers, and other single people. Soon there will be many persons in their seventies and eighties. As they age there will be increased demand for supportive services. The formal and informal supportive networks will become more important.

The Mobile or Trailer Home

Another option adopted by some retired couples is that of the mobile or trailer home. These are called that because they are prefabricated in a factory, built on wheels, and designed to be towed behind a tractor. So far they are not taxed as real estate but as a motor vehicle.

They may be moved to a small lot. They may be placed on a corner of a son or daughter's property. More typically they are moved to a rented lot in a trailer park where they are blocked up off the wheels, more or less permanently installed. One owns the house but not the lot. One pays rent for the lot; rent may be subject to escalation with inflation and increase in taxes. This is really a variant of the smaller house.

Mobile home parks vary greatly in the way they are developed and maintained. Some are little more than parking lots on the edge of a town with hook-ups for light and water, where trailers are set close together in minimal spaces. Some grow up haphazardly. Others are carefully planned. Some are laid out and landscaped beautifully. In some the trailers are set in shallow pits so they have the appearance of bungalows in city developments. Some are open to all ages. Others are limited to older people. Some have spacious clubhouses and recreational facilities. So a move to a trailer park may in some ways be a move to a resort community or to a planned retirement community. Usually they are available to a clientele less affluent than those of the planned retirement community.

There is a wide variety of choice and levels of cost in trailer homes. Also there tends to be a high rate of depreciation on the value of the home unless it is permanently installed, so that resale possibilities may be problematic. There have been some questions about the safety of mobile homes. They are vulnerable to high winds unless anchored. Some of them are not well insulated and may be hard to heat or cool. Many are a considerable distance from all kinds of services. One of their main advantages seems to be that a person can secure a fully equipped house at low cost and live fairly inexpensively in a trailer park.

The Motor Home

Although the motor home is basically a recreational vehicle, there are persons who have chosen to spend some retirement years in them. The motor home is not set down more or less permanently on blocks, but is ready to roll whenever the owner decides to leave. Often parked in a recreational vehicle park, it may be driven to state and national parks which have campgrounds for trailers, or even trailer parks which are located in almost every town of any size. It may even be set for a time in the driveway of a friend or relative.

Joe and Jan Johnson had always been outdoor people with an unfulfilled urge to travel. They took early retirement, sold the house and furniture, and bought a 32-foot motor home. During the first two years they saw much of the West and Canada, traveling north in summer and south in winter, staying in one place as long as they wanted. Finally they found a recreational vehicle park in the Southwest where they spend the winter months and another in the Northwest.

This is a gypsy existence. If a fuel shortage develops and as the cost of gasoline rockets, this mode of living may be priced out of existence for some, although there is a trend toward the development of mini-motor homes that are more economical to operate than the gigantic and luxurious land yachts.

Some of the commercially operated recreational vehicle parks which cater to retired persons entice customers with clubhouses and all sorts of recreational facilities. So this is another version of the resort or the retirement community.

Motor-home living may be a short-term mode of spending retirement. It may be an adjunct, a way of moving without dispensing with the old homestead. It may be a one-time fling. Those who opt for this mode trade space and privacy for mobility and a life out of doors in vacation country. Permanence and stability of relationships are traded for flexibility and variety.

5

Changing Living Arrangements: Regrouping

We may solve some of our housing problems by changing where we live. It is possible also to solve some of them by changing our living arrangements.

In the last chapter moving was termed *relocation*. A change in living arrangements will be designated here as *regrouping*. Here too there are varieties of possibilities.

Hiring Help

One obvious answer to the problem of maintaining a house and yard in the face of diminishing energy and strength is to hire others to do the more taxing tasks—mowing the lawn, shoveling snow, raking leaves, washing windows, doing heavy cleaning, rearranging furniture. To begin with, we might have someone come in for a few hours as needed to do the strenuous yard work or the heavy housecleaning. The next level would be to hire live-in help, serving as houseman, butler, maid, cook or chauffeur. This may be very satisfactory if the help is available. But hiring help can become very expensive. So it may be limited to those with considerable means.

In some communities organizations have developed various kinds of *home-care programs* and *home-health services*. Home-health services will be discussed in the following chapter on nursing care. Home-care services include meals-on-wheels, in which one hot meal is delivered to the home at least five days a week; usually the meals are planned under the supervision of a certified dietician with choices including low-fat, nonsalt and dietetic menus. Home-care services include handyman services in which retired craftsmen are available to perform minor repairs for small fees; new construction and ladder climbing are not included. Government assistance may be available for home repair and insulation for those on low income. Volunteer transportation to the store and to a physician's or dentist's office is provided by some organizations, as is assistance with shopping. Homemaker services in which trained persons come in a certain number of hours per week to clean, do laundry, change bedding, and cook food that can be warmed up on other days may be available for an hourly fee. Companion aid programs may offer company and support during times when one might otherwise have to be left alone.

Some of these services are supplied by volunteers. Some are paid for by the recipients. Some may be paid for out of community or government funds if the recipient is otherwise unable to afford them. These home care programs are designed to enable persons to maintain their independence and continue living in their own homes as long as it is appropriate to do so. They attempt to stave off unnecessary or too early institutionalization. They provide the kinds of supports that families often give to their older members to persons whose families may not be able to do this or to persons who have no families they can call on. Information about services available in your community may be obtained from information and referral centers or from social work agencies and senior centers.

Living with Children

Another solution is to live with children or have your children live with you.

A common image of the family is that of an elderly couple with several children who are grown up and married with families of their own, all living in the same community. A common expectation has been that when the elderly couple are unable to manage by themselves, or when one of them dies, they will move in with the children. If they do not move into the same house, they might move into an apartment nearby or into a suite of rooms in the house, sometimes spoken of as the "mother-in-law apartment."

Unfortunately, not all families are like that. There are older people who have never married. They may have lived by themselves for years or they may have doubled up with someone else. Even if married, not all couples have children, and of those who do there are some who outlive their children. Some families have scattered so that children live far away from the family homestead. Some parents and children have been estranged from each other and never communicate.

It is not uncommon for a retired couple to be assisting with the support of their own children, perhaps even their grandchildren. In fact, more aged parents are helping their grown children than the other way around.

Nor is it uncommon for retired persons to have their own parents still living.

There are a number of factors which make living with children in the later years problematic. The first one mentioned is that there may be no children to live with, although it is not uncommon for nieces and nephews to assume responsibility for an uncle or aunt.

Another factor is space, since many adult children are living in apartments or small houses with a minimum of extra room.

A third factor is money. Our system of public assistance

does not encourage families to take care of their elderly who have exhausted their funds, as assistance is available for living alone or in retirement and nursing homes but not if one lives in the family.

The biggest factor is a desire for independence. Most older people strongly prefer not to live with their children. Many would choose a nursing home rather than to move in on their children. It is a rare household where two generations, and even rarer when three generations, can live comfortably together with each generation feeling that it has a secure and important place in the family, allowed to participate fully in family decisions.

Contrary to popular myth, the three-generation family has never been common in America. When three generations have lived together in one house, it has been mainly because of economic necessity. The more common pattern is for family members to live nearby, for the grandparents to have a little house on the family farm, or for "mother-in-law apartments" attached as wings to houses. Also it is one thing for adult children to live with their parents, which was common a generation ago, and another thing for an elderly parent to live in the home of a son or daughter.

One of the barriers between the generations arises out of the social mobility of so many Americans in which the younger generation moves up the social scale and into a different social class, taking on a different life-style. For the generations to live together successfully there must have been a long history of close communication and constant relationships with the maintenance of common interests, values, and style of living. When parents have abused, neglected, ignored, or exploited their children, it is almost inevitable that the tables will be turned in the later years. Where parents and their children have drifted apart, it is very difficult to reestablish relationships in the later years. We are becoming increasingly aware of elderly who are physically as well as psychologically abused by relatives. Parent abuse is the other side of the coin from all too common child abuse.

To reestablish relationships or to make a decision about moving in with the children it is important to discuss feelings openly and to face the problems that have to be resolved. It is important for all parties to be clear about the expectations of the relationship.

House Sharing

In some cases when an older person possesses a house or even rents an apartment but has no relatives who can move in, it may be possible to work out a house-sharing arrangement with persons who are congenial. For example, it might be possible to make arrangements with a younger couple, perhaps even a couple in early retirement, who would be willing to move in, either to share expenses of maintaining the home or to provide services in lieu of paying rent. Quite often persons who live near campuses arrange to have students live in. Another example would be for several elderly persons to go together to develop a communal living arrangement, sharing responsibility for paying rent, for housekeeping, cooking, eating together, but with private bedrooms.

It is true that older people value privacy. But some might be willing to give up some privacy for the sake of companionship and safety. Since nearly 75% of the elderly own their own homes and many of these are under used, with probably 50% of them having three or more rooms per person, this seems to promise a solution to housing problems for the young, only about 6% of whom have this luxury, as well as for the old.

The important thing here is to explore and determine congeniality, what alteration of living patterns would have to be worked out, and what the arrangements and expectations will be. Values and style of living need to be discussed. A careful interview, personal references, and trial periods would be in order. House sharing calls for a process akin to courtship before entering it. It works only when the persons involved are willing to trade some privacy for companionship and economy and are able to get along well with other persons.

In some communities there are organizations working to match congenial and compatible persons so they can share a house. Project SHARE in Nassau County, New York, Project MATCH in San Jose, California, Shared Housing Program in Duluth, Minnesota, and Share-A-Home Associations with headquarters in Winter Park, Florida, have come to my attention. In Kansas City the Share-A-Home Project is administered by a community college. Studies indicate that about a third of all older people are favorably inclined to the idea. This is not surprising when we remember that many college students and young working people have had the experience of teaming up to share housing and even more have lived in dormitory situations.

If this solution seems promising to you, you might call your local information and referral center, family service society, Community Chest or council of social agencies to see if a program exists in your area. If no program exists, you might appeal to your church either to start such a program or to put you in touch with others who are similarly inclined. Some senior centers have bulletin boards where your interest can be posted. In fact, your local senior center might be encouraged to set up such a service.

Success and happiness in the relationship in house-sharing, as in marriage or business partnerships, depend upon the compatibility of the persons involved, their skill in developing relationships with other persons, and their willingness to compromise for the sake of companionship. If you have relatives or friends with whom you get along well who are also interested, you might have a head start on this solution.

Senior Citizen Apartments

In almost every community there are apartment complexes constructed especially for senior citizens and persons with handicapping conditions. Most of them are high-rise buildings, although some are in the form of separate cottages or garden apartments. They run the gamut from luxury apartments to low-income subsidized housing. Some have been built for profit by private developers. Others are constructed by nonprofit corporations sponsored by churches. Many are public housing, constructed and operated under government auspices. In some cases they have been developed by remodeling old hotels and office buildings. In most cases they are new structures.

The senior-citizen apartment is an option for either a married couple or a single person. Usually such complexes contain efficiency apartments or one-bedroom apartments. If they are erected with the assistance of low-interest, government-guaranteed loans to the buildings, they must meet certain requirements. The major requirement is that a certain proportion of these units must go to elderly persons who are on low incomes and who will not pay rent of more than 25 % of their income. In addition to apartments equipped with safety features desirable for older people, these are protected-access buildings to deter crime, and someone is on duty 24 hours a day in case of emergencies.

Most senior-citizen apartment complexes have public rooms where meetings can be held. Some have activity directors and organized social programs. In others the programs are sponsored by volunteer organizations.

Some are located convenient to shopping centers, transportation lines, and other community services. Some are isolated. Some have trained and compassionate management. In others the quality of management leaves something to be desired.

The number of social services and the attention given to developing activities for residents vary considerably according to the state and to the commitment of the management of the facilities. Some space for public meetings and social events is planned in the building, but sometimes this is minimal. Sometimes outside organizations assume responsibility for providing social and counseling services in these facilities. Many are near centers which provide services such as a daily hot meal at low cost, recreational activities, and health clinics.

Those who can afford luxury housing probably can find it in almost every city. Unfortunately low-cost housing is in very short supply, and waiting lists are long. As you learn about such housing under construction, you might investigate and see if you can get your name on the waiting list. In some cases persons with special needs may be given priority.

Retirement Hotels

Another possibility is a retirement hotel. In many cities older downtown hotels have been converted to retirement hotels catering almost exclusively to retired persons. These are what the name implies. They rent rooms or suites of rooms by the month. They provide furnishings, linens, and housekeeping services as in a transient hotel. They maintain a restaurant or dining room on the premises where payment is by the meal or on a weekly or monthly basis. Except for the fact that the management may be ready to give assistance in an emergency, such as calling an ambulance, they may take little or no responsibility for any other kinds of services or programs. They are strictly places to live with a minimum of effort spent on housekeeping.

They vary greatly in terms of cost and quality of accommodations offered. Some are swank, beautiful, and exclusive. Some are run-down fleabags offering single-room occupancy cheaply to drifters. If no effort is spent on developing social programs or community activities, if one has no friends, these can be lonely places. However, being let alone is something which some persons prefer. They like retirement-hotel living precisely because no one bothers them, and they do not have to be involved with other people.

If support services such as transportation, medical care, social centers, and churches are accessible, this may make all the difference in the world.

Entering a Retirement Home

Another possibility is to apply for admission to a retirement home which provides congregate living. Homes may be operated by a corporation that is associated with or sponsored by a religious denomination or a fraternal association, or by a for-profit corporation. Such homes usually offer a continuum of services representing levels of care all the way from (1) independent living in a cottage to (2) congregate living which includes taking one's meals in a common dining room to (3) aid for daily living or the provision of personal services such as help with dressing, assistance with hygiene, and surveillance of medication to (4) skilled nursing care. Usually a nursing staff is on duty and on call 24 hours a day. Usually each living unit has an emergency call system. Many have a residents' organization that takes responsibility, with assistance from the staff, for developing all kinds of activities and social events. A big selling feature of the retirement home is that one is assured of being able to secure the level of care one needs at the time the need arises, and one can move back and forth between levels of care provided in the same location. However, not all do offer all these levels of care. It is important to check this out.

In their middle seventies Ellen and Edgar Dickson decided to move into an apartment in a retirement home. They prepared their own breakfast and supper but ate their main meal in the community dining room. They were not far from their children. If they wanted to serve a company dinner in their apartment, they could do so, or they could reserve a private dining room at the community center. Edgar continued to attend Rotary. Ellen was active in the women's organization of the church. Their golden wedding celebration was held in the community center.

When Edgar died, Ellen was not left alone. She had friends to visit and eat with. She had easy access to a multitude of activities. She had the privacy of her own apartment and the security of knowing that if she got sick help was close at hand and immediately available.

Such homes have to be judged not only by the physical surroundings and the social services they provide, but also by the spirit and culture of the community. One advantage they offer is that they can cater to a particular religious or ethnic community, although most of them are nondenominational and open to all without discrimination.

More and more privately developed for-profit retirement homes are being built. They vary from modest facilities which can be afforded by persons on Supplemental Security Income payments to luxurious complexes.

Retirement homes appeal to persons—married couples or singles—who are looking for companionship and easy access to group activities as well as assurance of life care on one campus or in one community.

Retirement homes featuring congregate living are not to be confused with rest homes or nursing homes. Although most retirement homes have infirmaries and some even have nursing facilities on the grounds, these are designed for residents who may become ill. The main emphasis in retirement homes is on providing convenient access to social activities, on companionship, on security, and on the availability of a continuum of care in meeting changing needs all in one location.

Entrance into a retirement home is not to be confused with being "put away" by the family. Most homes refuse to take persons who are not themselves actively desirous of entering. It is not a retreat from life. Residents are encouraged to maintain ties and involvement in community organizations. Residents are free to come and go as they please just as in their own homes. Some residents even hold part-time jobs while living in retirement homes.

The advantages of living in a retirement home are that they provide companionship. A person does not have to eat alone. They provide support. One does not have to do the heavy housecleaning or laundry, because these are taken care of. One can be involved in social activities without going outside the home. Many such homes have chapels and social halls where concerts, religious services, parties, and classes are held. They provide security and safety with call systems in the rooms and nursing assistance constantly available in emergencies.

There are, of course, disadvantages to living in a retirement home. A resident needs to conform to an institution's schedule of meals, although many have somewhat flexible hours. Menus may become monotonous. Living in close proximity to others may be wearing, even though one's own room is private.

The chief disadvantage of the retirement home may lie in the method of financing. Most require a lump-sum accommodation fee or entrance fee or founder's fee which is, in effect, rent paid in advance. It buys the accommodation, which belongs to one as long as one lives and then reverts to the home when one dies. If one lives out one's expected span, this may be a bargain. If one dies soon after entering, money that might have gone to an estate goes to the home. In this case, what one does in effect is to make a gift to the home which enables it to serve others in return for the insurance it provides. In addition to the accommodation fee there is usually a monthly maintenance fee which goes for food, housekeeping services, use of public rooms, administration, and social services.

In the past some of these homes got into financial difficulty because they collected a one-time lump sum in exchange for a promise to take care of all expenses of the member for life, without taking sufficient account of possible inflation. Occasionally they failed to maintain a reserve large enough to be able to refund unused portions of accommodation fees if persons elected to leave within a five-year period. Now many include an escalation clause in the contract which enables them to set the monthly fee to cover the cost. Now some of these homes are adopting the condominium plan in which one buys a living unit.

Persons interested in such homes should have financial statements and a detailed contract to examine. It is good to have legal or financial advice before signing a contract which entails more than a monthly maintenance fee. New laws and regulations make abuses of the consumer far less likely now, although even in the past the number of problem situations has been small.

The financial status and management record of privately run retirement homes is important to know, even if one does not pay an advanced fee.

Most homes welcome—and some insist on—a trial period before a contract is signed. In any case it is best to visit, to talk with those who live there, and if at all possible to spend a few days living there to experience the flavor of the home and to see if one can be comfortable there.

6

When
Nursing Care
Is Needed

All of us hope that we can avoid serious illness, that we can be spared agonizing pain, and that we can escape being a patient in a hospital. However, as we grow older, the probabilities of facing such experiences increase markedly. In 1976, for example, older people had around a one-in-six chance of being hospitalized during the year as compared with a one-in-ten chance for persons under 65 years of age.

Since any of us may need intensive care for heart trouble or major surgery, we are grateful for the availability of good hospitals. Only those who have spent time in some of the so-called developing nations really understand how fortunate we are to have health facilities we so casually take for granted. In the meantime, as we learn more about the importance of diet and exercise, learn to avoid dangerous habits, and develop new medicines and means of treatment, we may be able to reduce our chances of being a hospital patient.

Hospitals can be frightening places to enter, especially if we have never been a patient. When we enter, we put ourselves into the hands of strangers. New and mysterious routines go on around us. We are apprehensive about the unknown, concerned about the prognosis of our disease. We dread the thought of pain endured in examinations, diagnosis, and treatment.

We are fortunate if we have physicians, nurses, and attendants who are willing to take time to explain what they are going to do and why. We are fortunate if they are honest with us and let us know what our situation is and what we can expect. If we do find ourselves in a situation where our need to know is overlooked, we may have to be more aggressive about asking questions. Many hospitals are now putting patient advocates on the staff to assist patients to get answers to their questions and attention to their needs. Social workers and chaplains, as well as our own pastor, may help us to deal with our fears and anxieties.

After hospitalization for serious illness or for surgery comes a period of convalescence. Sometimes this is merely a matter of allowing time for healing, and during the convalescent period we can have all our needs met at home, although we may have to go back to a clinic or the physician's office to have dressings changed and to be checked for progress. If we live with others, they may be able to provide all the support we need and do for us those things which we cannot do for ourselves for a while. If we live alone, others may come in to be with us temporarily. Or we may be able to arrange for home health services, such as visiting nurses who come to give medication, assist with baths, and change bandages.

However, if we live alone and if home health care services cannot do all that is needed, we may have to spend some time in a convalescent hospital. This is true especially if we need to assist convalescence by rehabilitation procedures. For example, for a time we may not be able to get out of bed and walk unassisted. We may have to have knowledgeable support while we gain strength a little at a time in carefully graduated periods. We may have to be taught how to walk or talk again. We may have to learn how to use prosthetic devices. Exercises may be needed to increase our range of motion.

The decision on whether to recover in one's own home rather than go to a convalescent hospital depends on a number of factors. One is the severity of one's disability during the period of convalescence and the amount of nursing care needed. If one can dress oneself, is ambulatory, and has few special dietary or medical problems, this is one thing. If one requires a great deal of assistance for a while and has to be kept under the watch of trained attendants, that is another.

A second factor is the safety and convenience of the home itself where climbing stairs or being out of reach of a telephone may preclude staying at home. If the home is too far removed from the physician's office and travel is arduous, that will enter into the decision.

A third factor is the presence of other persons who can and are willing to provide the needed nursing care without undue strain or serious disruption of their lives and relationships.

A fourth factor is the availability of home health care services. The decision of where to spend your convalescence is usually made in consultation with the attending physician and perhaps the hospital social-service department.

Home Health Care Services

There is increasing interest in providing health care to persons in their own homes in order to avoid the trauma of institutionalization and with the hope that home care may be less expensive as well as more appropriate. Programs vary widely from state to state and from community to community. Here are some of the things to check out:

1. Policies Supporting Home Care

As this is written, Medicare and Medicaid as well as tax policies tend to favor hospitalization and institutional care.

But these policies are being changed so that certain kinds of services may be reimbursed by Medicare and Medicaid if delivered to the home. Proposals currently being discussed include payment to relatives or family members for taking care of an older person at home or allowing tax deductions for the care of a relative. Each of us has a stake in the formulation of these policies.

2. Programs of Home Health Care

One of the oldest, best known and most common home health aids is that of the visiting nurse who comes to the home to give injections, oversee medications, counsel on health problems, and check on health status by taking blood pressure, pulse, and temperature. A visiting nurse may also change dressings and give baths.

Physical therapists may be available to give treatments in the home.

Speech therapists may help those whose ability to talk has been impaired by a stroke to talk again.

Companion aides who have been screened and trained for their jobs may be hired to come in at times to relieve other members of the family. They may also do minor chores.

Friendly visitors may relieve the tedium.

Volunteers may be prepared to provide transportation to the physician's office or to the hospital for out-patient treatments.

There are telephone reassurance systems in which one receives a call at a specified time each day to be sure the patient can answer and is getting along all right. If the call is not answered, emergency procedures are activated. There are other systems in which a person can carry a small device that can dial a telephone number by remote control or automatically signal an answering service if the patient were to fall and black out.

Day Care Centers or Day Hospitals

To support or supplement the family which tries to care at home for a person who is either convalescent or suffers from a chronic handicapping condition, some communities have established day-care programs in which the person is brought to a center during the day. The family provides care at night. The center, administered by a trained staff, provides from one to three meals a day, supervises medications, and may even provide physical therapy in addition to social activities. These are especially helpful to the family, such as the single woman trying to care for her mother, who must go out to work during the day.

If these centers are conceived primarily as day hospitals, they will be committed to an emphasis on rehabilitation. Persons will be referred to them by a physician. They are short-term programs which attempt to bring persons to the point where they can be discharged as recovered. If they are conceived as day-care centers, they will emphasize social services; they will see themselves as basically custodial; and they will work with the persons on a long-term basis.

The per-day cost of day care is about half of that in the Intermediate Care Facility. This enables limited assets to go much further, as well as to keep patients domiciled in their own homes. The most successful day-care centers provide transportation. A patient is picked up in the morning, escorted to the center and returned home at night. If family members have to provide the transportation, this may either be impossible or too burdensome.

Residential and Nursing Care

Up to this point we have been talking about episodic illness and convalescence. The illness may put us in a hospital, and convalescence may require us to spend some time in a convalescent facility, but eventually we go back home. Now we come to cases where our illness or accident may have been of such a nature that we will never completely recover. We will have to cope with a handicapping condition for the rest of our life, and we may need nursing care on a daily basis. If our chronic illness or permanent disability is of such nature that we need aid with daily living or nursing care, and if we do not have families who can care for us, even with the aid of home health services or day care, then we may become a long-term resident of a nursing home.

The first thing to point out is that there are different kinds of nursing homes, to use the term loosely, according to the kind of care they are equipped to give. Here, as in housing, there is a wide range of options to choose from in meeting a variety of needs. Look for the option which is appropriate to current need as well as the one most desirable in other respects, such as location, cost, and cultural orientation.

1. Residential Care

At the beginning level there are board-and-care homes, sometimes popularly known as "rest homes," sometimes designated as "group homes for adults." Basically these are little more than the old-fashioned boarding house except that in most places they are now required to have a special license and they may be in a building especially designed rather than in someone's big old house.

In addition to board and room they may provide aid to daily living, such as helping persons with bathing, grooming, and dressing, keeping an eye on them to see if they are comfortable, and reminding them to take medicines. In short, they generally do for an older person what a grown son or daughter might do. They should meet minimum standards for health and safety. They are inspected regularly by licensing agencies who monitor compliance with regulations and standards.

They do not need to provide a registered nurse. They are not allowed to give medications. They focus on the social rather than medical needs and emphasize the resident's status as "resident" rather than as "patient."

2. Intermediate Care Facilities (ICFs)

On the second level there are nursing homes, or wings of nursing homes, that take only persons who need a limited amount of nursing care. Usually they are required to have a registered nurse available for consultation as well as a physician to serve as medical director on a part-time basis, particularly if they are certified to receive Medicare or Medicaid reimbursement. Licensed vocational nurses, or as they are called in some states, licensed practical nurses, are on the staff at all times. They are trained to give medications as prescribed by physicians and to check for vital signs such as blood pressure, pulse, and temperature. Sometimes these intermediate-care facilities are referred to as "infirmaries," especially if they are connected with a retirement community.

Most homes of this sort are not able to take persons who are alcoholic or addicted to drugs. Nor can they accept those who are seriously disturbed. There are special facilities for such persons. Basically an intermediate care facility is equipped to give more health care than the residential care facility, but the emphasis still is more on social than medical needs. Persons needing custodial care more than nursing care are candidates for this level of care.

Good intermediate care facilities will work to keep the surroundings homelike rather than like a hospital. They will provide occupational therapy and recreational activities. They will attempt, if not to restore lost functions, to enable the residents to preserve those functions they have by keeping as active as possible; so they will plan activities such as parties and excursions.

3. Skilled Nursing Facilities (SNFs)

On the third level of care, there are skilled nursing facilities which are prepared to provide almost every kind of nursing care short of intensive or post-operative care. Generally they do not have operating rooms or physicians in residence, as hospitals do. Registered nurses are in charge and required to be on duty at least one full shift, although some have registered nurses on duty 24 hours a day.

Persons who are confined to bed and have to be turned regularly, who are incontinent and have to be changed and kept clean frequently, persons who must have help in eating, and persons who need intravenous medication or feeding—these persons need skilled nursing care. Often this is long-term care with medical problems outweighing the social needs.

Skilled nursing facilities are prepared to give rehabilitation therapies and should be committed to the restoration of function if at all possible. Therefore they are often called "convalescent hospitals" rather than "nursing homes." The need of long-term care patients for companionship, diversion, and social services is still crucial. Also they should be concerned about maintaining as much function as possible, even when restoration is impossible.

In such homes one finds seriously ill and badly deteriorated persons as well as those who are on their way to being discharged. Generally an attempt is made to keep these separated in different sections. The picture is further confused because some facilities offer both intermediate care and skilled nursing care separated only into different wings and by different rates for each level.

4. Specialized Nursing Care

Many hospitals have special departments or wards for persons afflicted with mental illness, addicted to drugs, or suffering from alcoholism. In addition there are special treatment centers for such persons, some residential and some offering out-patient care. It may be difficult to find placement for the older person with such special health problems, inasmuch as many of these places prefer not to treat older persons on the ground they are not amenable to treatment.

However, some nursing homes have special licenses and special wards for the care of persons with these problems. There may be some state institutions to care for them.

Oh, No! Not a Nursing Home!

With this brief description of the kinds and levels of nursing care, we come to a discussion of the emotions which cluster around nursing homes, amounting to fear and revulsion. These emotions are exacerbated by occasional exposés of abuses and fraud which have been discovered in some nursing homes. Are these negative feelings justified? Are there substitutes for or alternatives to nursing homes which would make them unnecessary?

Obviously none of us looks forward to being sick and disabled. None of us relishes the prospect of a trip to the hospital because of serious illness. Even less do we anticipate the prospect of ending our days in a condition of helplessness, pain, or senility. Worst of all is the prospect of having to live out our lives away from home and family in an institution.

There is the possibility that our feelings about nursing homes are not commensurate with the reality. It may be that our anticipation colors our experience when we do have to go to one. Let's explore these feelings a bit more.

Some of the negative feelings may stem from the confusion of the contemporary nursing home with the old "poor farm." Until the middle of this century it was expected that the old and the sick would be taken care of by their families. When persons without families grew old and sick and there was no one to take care of them and they had no money to pay others for taking care of them, the only available care was the "alms house," "poor farm," or "work house" maintained by towns or counties. If they were confused, disoriented, or disturbed there was a good chance they would be sent to a state hospital for the mentally ill. Before 1950 37% of the institutionalized elderly were in mental hospitals. By 1970 this had dropped to 8%, while 60% were in nursing homes. Both the poor farms and the mental hospitals were usually located in out-of-the-way places where respectable people would not have to see them or associate with their residents. Frequently these were working farms where residents and patients earned part of their keep by working as much as they could in the fields, stables, and shops.

After 1935, when Social Security became available and Old Age Assistance money was provided for those whose income from Social Security was too small or who were not eligible for Social Security, more and more older people became capable of paying for care. Also, the concept became more widespread that older people were entitled to be cared for by the community if they could not care for themselves. Demands arose for more humane and higher quality care for the aged. The county poor farms were either phased out or metamorphosed into nursing homes giving better care. At the same time a number of persons with big houses and unoccupied rooms began to take in older boarders who could pay out of Old Age Assistance. These are sometimes spoken of as the "Mom and Pop" facilities—the forerunner of the modern nursing home. Some gave excellent and compassionate care. Others took advantage of their elderly charges. As the number of persons in these places increased and more persons became aware of them, more stringent health and safety regulations were passed and stricter licensing requirements were imposed, so that these small makeshift homes gradually gave way to larger, better constructed, more professionally run homes.

Then in 1966 Medicare and Medicaid were established. For the first time large amounts of money became available for the care of the sick and frail elderly. There was need for many more facilities. Private enterprise was attracted to what is now spoken of as the "health industry." Nursing homes became good investments. Today most of the nursing homes are proprietary institutions, developed by investors who expect to make a profit from the operation.

The health care industry grew so rapidly that the machinery and the will for regulating and operating the programs of federal and state funding hardly had time to be worked out. Between 1966 and 1976 the number of nursing home residents increased 245%. Consequently there were abuses by unscrupulous operators who tried to maximize profits by keeping costs as low as possible and manipulating bookkeeping methods to secure as high a rate of reimbursement as possible. At the same time the number of trained and experienced administrators were few. But most operators struggled to provide the best care they could while living with rapidly changing standards, emerging new medical technologies, and constantly changing regulations in the face of accelerating inflation. Stricter licensing of administrators and requirements for training are constantly raising the level of competence of nursing-home staffs.

Currently, nursing-home standards are set by federal regulations governing institutions certified for Medicare reimbursement. Nursing-home rates are in effect set by what Medicaid will pay, since the great majority of older people in nursing homes are what is called "medically indigent." The exceptions to this are those nursing homes that refuse to accept Medicare or Medicaid and cater to more affluent clients.

In addition to federal regulations, the states drew up regulations covering those institutions which do not apply for Medicare and Medicaid certification.

As a result modern nursing homes are usually quite different from the stereotypes based on earlier situations.

Some of our negative feelings may be tied up with the lingering social norm that children or other family members should care for their parents and older relatives, so there is guilt and shame on the part of the children as well as resentment and a feeling of rejection on the part of older people when their children do not take them in, even if they are not able to. When we are sick, we want to have those we love and who love us near. Especially then we want to be in our own home with our own family.

Some of the fear of the nursing home may be based on the assumption that once you go into a nursing home you never leave. Entering the nursing home therefore is the beginning of the end, which is death. It is true that in their last months a number of older people become patients in nursing homes. But it is true also that for many a nursing home is a way-station where they can recover between the acute hospital and their own homes. In other words, if one's health improves, as it may, especially if the nursing facility is committed to rehabilitation, one may leave for housing that is suited to the current condition. If health does not improve, then one may be fortunate to have a haven where good care is provided.

But perhaps more of the horror of the nursing home grows out of the fact that one sees there many very ill and disabled persons. As long as one is in a hospital, there is a lingering hope for recovery. But when long-term care of very ill persons is indicated, hope gives way to helpless waiting. Many of the illnesses encountered in a nursing home are caused by the so-called degenerative diseases which are irreversible in nature and which tend to be more common among the very old. One sees there patients confined to wheelchairs or who are bedfast. Some may have suffered from strokes which have left them confused or disabled. Some may be unable to feed themselves and must be fed by others. Some are incontinent, which con-tributes to a bad odor. These are not pretty sights. They remind all of us of our own rapidly approaching old age, of our own inescapable death. So to some of us the terror of degeneration, the recoil from pain, the anxiety about death is transferred to the nursing home and the staff. If we did not have to look at these things, we could put them out of our mind. When we see them, we are angry that they have to be and that they cannot be cured.

To the extent that living in an institutional setting isolates persons from the larger world, deprives them of the power to control their own destinies, consigns them to a lower status, reduces the amount of stimulation received from the environment, takes away privacy, and violates dignity, it tends to dehumanize people. The better institutions try to keep such tendencies to a minimum. Respect for persons, compassion for their situation, and sensitivity to their needs should impel all of us to break down institutional barriers between persons and the community.

However, it must be pointed out that poverty, illness, and loss of capacity to function may do all of these things to persons while they are living in their own homes. Any living arrangement involves a trade-off between goods. So care in a well-managed nursing home may be better and preferable to anything available outside in the light of circumstances. It may provide safety and security that would not be available elsewhere and, by supporting the resident, provide more freedom to function than if they were to be in less sheltered quarters.

There is another factor in our fear of the nursing home. All of us have been schooled to be independent and to stand on our own feet. From very early childhood we fight to maintain our autonomy and assert our competence. We have been made to feel guilty if we were an unnecessary burden on others. One of the hardest things to bear is helplessness and utter dependence on the good will or willingness of others to meet our needs. We can stand it for a short time if we are sure we will recover. But when we know that we will not recover, it may become an intolerable imprisonment among strangers. It is hard not to feel rejected by family and abandoned by friends, especially if we are removed from them geographically and they are so involved with their own affairs they have little time to spend with us or if they are repelled by the atmosphere of the home and find it easy to put off going to see us.

Truly, the nursing home can be a kind of captivity or exile. We can lament with the Psalmist:

> By the waters of Babylon,
> there we sat down and wept,
> when we remembered Zion.
> On the willows there
> we hung up our lyres.
>
> .   .   .   .   .
>
> How shall we sing the Lord's song
> in a foreign land? (Psalm 137:1-2, 4)

Is there a way to avoid going to a nursing home? Are there real alternatives? The answer has to be *maybe. Yes* and *No.*

Alternatives to Institutional Care

It is difficult to know how many older persons are living in nursing homes who do not need the kind and quality of care which a nursing home is set up to give. Various studies indicate that many are there because they need to be somewhere, and as there are no other facilities and sufficient supports in the community, this is the only choice. Just as many older people used to find their way to state mental institutions and before that to the poor farms, so now many find their way to nursing homes because the community has not yet invented or developed the kinds of social institutions needed to care for all the elderly.

The most obvious alternative to a nursing home is a family that is able and willing to care for the older person at home, either by moving in with them or by taking them into their own. It is impossible to estimate how many children are doing this because they believe it is the most loving thing to do, because it is their duty, and because they believe they can afford both the physical effort and the monetary cost of doing it. In some cases this works out all right. But in other cases it exacts a heavy toll on those giving the care, leading even to physical breakdown or to the breakup of the family itself. Studies indicate that families do not abandon their elderly, if the elderly have families. In fact, even to those who are in nursing homes, the amount of time, attention, and care devoted by their relatives is impressive and often unappreciated.

The other obvious alternative is that of home care services and day-care centers. These services may support and supplement the care given by the family. They may make the difference between being able to keep the older person in the home and not. In some cases they enable the older person, even without family, to continue living in his or her own home longer. Every effort ought to be made to develop supplementary and supportive services in every community in view of the fact that the modern family has changed in structure and size so that it is no longer strong enough to provide care by itself. It should be noted, however, that home care may not be as economical as its proponents believe, and it may confirm a person in isolation. We need more experimentation to see what we can do.

If the family is not able to provide nursing care, if home care services are insufficient, and if the condition of the older person calls for constant and competent care, the nursing home may be the only appropriate facility.

From the Children's Point of View

When the relationship between an older parent and a grown child has been close, where there are strong ties of affection, and where over the years they have shared much of their life together, the family may choose to care for the older person in their own home. This can be an enriching even though toilsome experience for both generations. When the relationship has not been close or positive, the care of an older person at home may be an intolerable burden. Parents who have exploited, neglected, or abused their children when they were young may not expect the children to be devoted to them when they come to the end of their lives. When the burden of care falls mainly on a member of the family not related, such as a daughter-in-law, or the financial responsibility rests on a son-in-law, the situation is even worse.

It is very difficult for a grown child to watch progressive deterioration in one whom he or she loves. Forgetfulness, confusion, incontinence, loss of fastidiousness, loss of ability to communicate divest the parent or older friend of the charm, dignity, power, and spirit that once characterized them. Anguish over the progressive loss of an important relationship, distress over the demeaning condition to which illness reduces the parent, anxiety about becoming the head of the clan, and guilt about not being able to do more for the parent are common feelings.

Love for parents and human responsibility may require that the parents be assisted to find a place where they can receive the care their condition demands, even if it turns out to be a nursing home.

Separation is part of the human experience. Separation from one set of relationships means taking up a new set of relationships. As persons change, our relationship to them must change also. The nursing home is a kind of community with new neighbors as well as a formal network of supportive services.

Entry of a parent into a nursing home does not need to mean a break with the family. Families can and do visit. In one nursing home a sister came every day to sit for a couple of hours with her sister who had suffered a stroke that left her unresponsive. The healthy sister combed her sick sister's hair, saw to it that she was properly clothed, and helped to feed her lunch. Families can provide many services such as reading, writing letters, running errands, and so on. Studies have shown that family relationships often improve when the older person enters a nursing home.

Fortunately, churches and other organizations are beginning to become concerned to surround patients in nursing homes with the kind of personal care and humane treatment which makes life bearable there. Volunteers can be organized to supplement the care given by paid staff. Omsbudsmen and advocates can be vigilant to see that patients are not abused, neglected, or exploited, that they receive the treatment they deserve and have paid for, that their rights are respected, and that they are treated as persons of value. If the community can overcome its prejudice against the nursing home, it can move more positively to make the nursing home part of the community and to focus on making it a home—even if the last home—for many.

Choosing a Nursing Home

Nursing homes vary in the quality of care they provide and in the atmosphere with which the patient is surrounded. The choice of a nursing home is an important part of the care. This choice is made the same way one chooses any other residence.

The first step is to determine, usually in consultation with the physician or a social worker, the kind of care the older person needs. Any special limitations or requirements for treatment have to be considered in addition to the level of nursing care.

Concurrently, one has to assess both assets and limitations. What one can pay now and how one will finance nursing care is crucial. It may determine whether we get a private room, a semiprivate room, or a bed in a ward, although these are related to physical condition as well as to cost. If we want to continue under the care of a particular physician, we must go where that physician is willing and able to attend us. If frequent visits are expected from the family, the location of the home is important.

Armed with this kind of information, the next step is to check out and preferably to visit available homes. The Yellow Pages of the telephone directory contain names, addresses, and numbers of nursing homes. Their ads sometimes show pictures. Some homes advertise in the newspapers, especially when first opened. Physicians and social workers will be familiar with certain homes. Information and referral centers, medical societies, and health and welfare departments of cities will have lists.

We will want to be assured that the home is properly licensed and accredited. This information should be prominently displayed in the home itself as well as shared with us by the management. There are two kinds of accreditation. One is called Peer Accreditation by fellow members of an association which sets voluntary standards for its membership. There are denominational associations, professional associations, and associations of proprietary homes such as that of the American Health Care Association. There are also state associations.

The other form of accreditation is by the Joint Commission on Accreditation of Hospitals based on onsite surveys to check compliance with the Commission's standards. If the home is certified to receive Medicare and Medicaid reimbursement, it will have passed a rigorous inspection by the state licensing agency to see that it complies with federal as well as state regulations governing eligibility.

We will want to know about the ownership and the sponsorship of the home, whether a proprietary or a nonprofit facility. Many states require that this information be prominently posted. If it is not, we will inquire. A reliable and stable ownership by experienced operators assures one of a continuing level of care. Sponsorship by fraternal or religious bodies may tell us something of the cultural orientation and social atmosphere as well as provide some insurance of its integrity of purpose. However, the fact that a home is related to or sponsored by a fraternal or religious organization does not mean that these bodies control the home or assume responsibility for its financial integrity. It may mean that voluntary contributions are made by these bodies to support the home and that they have some interest in providing a ministry in the home.

We will also want to know something about the management. The administrator should be licensed. In some cases the administrator may be highly trained. In some cases the administrator will be a member of the College of Nursing Home Administrators. Information about these items may be displayed in the administrator's office.

We will be interested in the staff generally. Are they friendly? Do they seem dedicated to service? Is their relation to the patients respectful, concerned, and competent? The difference between a happy home and a sullen one can almost be felt by one who is sensitive to these things.

The general appearance of the home tells us much. Is it clean, attractive, free from most unpleasant odors, in good repair? Is it orderly?

A consumer's guide for choosing a long-term care facility entitled "Thinking About A Nursing Home" can be obtained from the American Health Care Association (see Appendix), any of their state chapters and from many homes belonging to the association. It provides a checklist of things to consider under 40 different categories. Similar lists from other organizations might be found.

The National Retired Teachers Association (NRTA) has published an excellent guide called "Selecting A Nursing Home." It can be obtained from any regional office of the AARP/NRTA or by writing to The National Retired Teachers Association at 1909 K Street N.W., Washington, D.C. 20049.

Before signing into a nursing home it is important to be clear about all the terms of the contract. We need to know what the basic rate is going to be and how it is to be paid. It is essential to understand what is included in that rate and what will be extra.

Living Victoriously in a Nursing Home

Moving into a nursing home is not the end of life but the beginning of a new period. It will be both opportunity and challenge. Unless you go into a home with which you are already familiar and in which some of your friends already live, you will be setting out to make a home in a new community among strangers. These are your new neighbors and may become your new friends. Some of them you will like immediately. Some will annoy you intensely. In a word, moving into a nursing home is not greatly different from moving into a house in another state or community except for two things. One is that you will be much more dependent on those around you for meeting your needs; you will have less control over what happens to you. The other is that the staff is there precisely to see that you are cared for.

So enter the home with the resolve to make the best of it. Go with the faith that God goes with you and that his Spirit is moving in the midst of it. Plan to make this your home. The attitude and spirit which you exhibit to others will be reflected back to you much of the time.

Be especially positive in your relationships with the employees. Try to know them as persons. Express appreciation to them for their services. They like to be appreciated. Try to understand their situation and their needs. Be aware of any cultural differences between their background and yours. If your home is in a small town, the staff may be made up of persons who have been your neighbors over the years. If it is in an urban area, you may know none of them and quite frequently they will be from other ethnic and minority groups.

The persons you will see most of and who will take care of you most often will be the nurse aides, the orderlies, and the housekeeping staff. They will do most of the hard and disagreeable things that have to be done around a nursing home such as changing beds which often are heavily soiled, giving baths, assisting persons to go to the toilet, mopping up spills and carrying trays, even feeding patients. Generally they will be too busy to spend much time visiting with you except in passing.

In most places they will be relatively unskilled workers, as they are called, except for those delicate skills of home-making and housekeeping which they learned in their own homes. However, increasingly requirements are being set for orientation and training of nurse aids so they may see them-selves as professionals, as they should. Generally they will be working for little more than minimum wages. Often they will be mothers who are the primary support of their families. Often they will be drawn from recent immigrant groups. They may go to a church different from yours. They may be devout Christians, or they may be alienated from any church. This may be your opportunity to gain insight into a different cultural community as well as to witness or to share to the power of Christian love.

You need to be aware that in addition to the nurse aides, who do most of the hard work, there are licensed vocational nurses (sometimes called licensed practical nurses) who have been trained to give medicines, take vital signs, and do many of the medical procedures. They will be in charge of a section of the home, working under the supervision of registered nurses who in turn are responsible to the attending physi-cians and the medical director. The administrator is respon-sible for staffing the home, for purchasing of supplies and services, for admissions, for inservice training of the staff, in short for the complete operation. Your physician is ulti-mately responsible for your physical care.

All of these are capable of compassion. Most of them will have some sense of dedication to their work. Many of them will see it as a kind of ministry. On the other hand, occa-sionally you will encounter an employee who is disinterested, incompetent, indifferent, lazy, or unreliable, as in any human community.

If you are contemptuous of persons from other races or

cultures or if you fear them, they will sense this. If you are squeamish about being touched by such persons, this will affect your relationships. If you are querulous, abusive, and unreasonably demanding, it will be harder for them to give you care. If, on the other hand, you are understanding, appreciative, and interested in them, generally they will respond.

However, you do have rights. In fact, these rights are spelled out in detail by licensing and certification agencies. You should have received a copy of them when you were admitted. Copies of the patient's bill of rights should be posted for all to see. Know your rights. Be assertive and firm in expecting what is due you even though you are not aggressive and impatient. You need not be passive in the face of neglect. You can resist either patronization or exploitation.

Try to find out and understand the reasons for the routines and the restrictions you may experience. Some of them may be for the convenience of the staff and the efficient (cost-effective) operation of the nursing home. Many of them are designed for your own protection and are in your interest. If they don't make sense to you or seem to fit your situation, you may be able to negotiate some flexibility in their application.

If you have problems or questions and you cannot get satisfaction from the aides or licensed nurses, ask to see the administrator. If you hesitate to do this or if it does not help, take up the matter with your physician. Some institutions have patient representatives on the staff to help you. Ombudsmen or visiting committees might help. Your pastor or a chaplain might counsel you on how to deal with the problems you face. One of the rights you have is to use the telephone and to communicate with anyone you wish. In fact, in most places there are consumer representatives you can call, and the licensing agency itself, usually the county or city department of health, can receive and must act on a complaint.

Keep in mind that even though you are in a nursing home and even though your strength and mobility have been greatly reduced, you are called to love God with all your being and your neighbor as yourself. You have a ministry. Here your neighbors are your fellow residents or patients, the nursing and housekeeping staff members, and the friends and family who come to see you. Through pain and in spite of disability you can witness to your faith, you can demonstrate what it means to be a human being and you can be loving toward those who serve you.

Clara, my wife's maiden aunt, a woman of education and culture, who had a long career as a public school teacher, finally found it wise to enter a nursing home. From this home she wrote, "Four of us get together once a week to share our experiences so we can keep on growing." In her last months she became increasingly weak. Her ability to see and hear and get around deteriorated. But to the very end she remained a gracious, thoughtful person, determined to remain as independent as possible. Sometimes she was confused and frightened, but in those dark times she held on to her faith.

Jewell, a distant relative, previously widowed, was partially paralyzed by a massive stroke which left her unable to talk coherently even though she understood perfectly what was going on around her. Although she spent the last six years of her life in a nursing home where she had to be lifted in and out of bed to a wheelchair, and in spite of her communication difficulties, she made of it a real home. She responded to those around her with affection. She exhibited a radiant countenance to all who came to see her. She lived each day as it came, appreciating the light and the flowers and human care until the day she died.

During their last years these persons, like many others, were a source of inspiration to all who knew them. Their memories linger on as examples of the power of a living faith.

7

Hospice
Care

Eventually, in accordance with God's plan for the universe he is creating, all of us will die. To some of us death will come suddenly and take us by surprise. But others of us may learn that we have a "terminal illness," which is to say that we are suffering from a disease which progresses rapidly and for which no cure is yet known. Therefore death is predictable within a matter of months. Although this may come as a shock, we will have been given the challenge and the privilege of living with dying. Of course, all of us are living with dying, for the life of each of us has a terminus. The difference is that for some of us death is assigned a much more definite date in the near future and we can measure the value of our remaining days. (See *Lving with Dying* by Glen W. Davidson, Minneapolis: Augsburg, 1975.)

Those of us who may have to cope with a foreseen and limited life span will then face a decision about how to spend those precious days and where to spend them. At that time we may turn for support to a hospice. Or it may be that our pastor or our physician or some of our friends will refer us to a hospice for counsel, comfort, and support. What is a hospice and how can it help us?

Basically, a hospice is a *concept* and an *attitude* about the care of the dying rather than a place where the dying are cared for. Also it is *persons* who have organized to provide such care.

Hospice care may be given in the patient's own home, for those who work with hospice believe that the last days of one's life ought to be as normal as possible and that one ought to be where family and friends can be with one as easily and as much as desired. It may be given in a special place built especially to provide a homelike setting for the dying. It may be given in a special wing of a hospital that has reorganized to make this kind of care possible.

Hospice care is based upon the recognition that while for most of us any prediction about the time of death is problematic, there are some of us who fall prey to diseases which can no longer be treated and whose progress will lead to death in the not too distant future. In other words it is care designed especially for those who have been diagnosed as "terminally ill" and who know they are faced with a limited span of life.

When that kind of diagnosis has been made, the hospice undertakes to assist the patient and his or her family to live the last days as fully as possible surrounded by those social supports which confirm personhood and human value. Treatment procedures that may be painful and demeaning as well as useless are discontinued. Medication is prescribed to insure that the patient does not experience unbearable pain and at the same time is not rendered senseless or confused. The commitment is that one does not need to die in pain and one does not need to die alone.

Hospice care, whether given at home or in an institution, is provided by an interdisciplinary team of professionals and lay volunteers, including the attending physician, nurses, social workers, clergy, and friends who are available to help the patient and the family in dealing with the situation. Members of this team are on call 24 hours a day. The physician, whether the family doctor or a specialist, normally is the director of the team. The coordination of the care given by the team may be delegated to another person, usually a trained nurse.

Formally, the term "hospice" has been defined by the Subcommittee on Health of the Interstate and Foreign Commerce Committee of the House of Representatives of the United States Congress in a "Discursive Dictionary of Health Care" as:

> as program which provides palliative and supportive care for terminally ill patients and their families, either directly or on a consulting basis with the patient's physician or another community agency such as a visiting nurse association. Originally a medieval name for a way station for pilgrims and travelers where they could be replenished, refreshed, and cared for; used here for an organized program of care for people going through life's last station. The whole family is considered the unit of care and care extends through the mourning process. Emphasis is placed on symptom control and preparation for and support before and after death, full scope health services being provided by an organized interdisciplinary team available on a twenty-four hour a day, seven day a week basis. Hospices originated in England (where there are about 24) and are now appearing in the United States.

As of this writing the number in the United States has expanded to more than 300, and others are in various stages of organization.

To recapitulate and review, a hospice has the following characteristics:

1. The primary unit of care is the terminally ill person and the family within the home, preferably, or in an institution if necessary, an institution especially set up for such care.

2. The physician is the director of an interdisciplinary care

team that provides the program of care which may draw on all the resources of the community.

3. Qualified volunteers may augment professionals in providing supportive services, perhaps drawing on friends and neighbors.

4. Services are available seven days a week on a 24-hour-a-day basis so neither the dying person nor the family needs to be alone if they do not wish to be.

5. The symptoms of the disease—physical, emotional, or spiritual—are dealt with and controlled as part of the program so that life may be not only endurable but also worth living.

6. A professional coordinates the day-to-day care program.

7. The supportive team meets to discuss concerns and to plan care in consultation with the family.

8. There is follow-up to deal with the bereavement and to support the family in doing their grief work.

9. Dying persons are assisted to live as fully and as comfortably as possible each remaining day rather than being prepared to die.

10. Hospice services are designed and given according to need.

The development of hospices is based upon a growing recognition that the hospital is geared primarily to treatment and cure of disease. The hospital environment tends to be stark and sterile. The routinization of procedures makes normal living difficult. When a patient has been diagnosed as terminally ill, all too often a subtle change in the relationship of the hospital staff to the patient takes place. Because of guilt over not being able to effect a cure or the fear of death itself, the staff may begin to avoid the patient, even to the point of neglect. The patient may be moved to a remote room and the door kept closed. So the patient is isolated. If the patient is put in intensive care, friends and family may be excluded much of the time. So while their needs for survival and safety may be met, their needs for human warmth, love, intimacy, affection, belonging, and self-actualization may not be.

In our society more and more persons have been separated from significant others in their lives, such as family and friends, when dying, just at the time they need and want support more than ever before. Hospice attempts to remedy that.

It has become difficult for Americans to face and to talk about death. Persons may need help to face it, to accept it, to communicate with each other about it and to live into it with faith and hope. Persons who have experienced being with the dying, who have come to terms with their own death, who know what bereavement feels like, and who have been trained to listen often are better able to support and comfort the dying and those around them. With support the last days can become rich and meaningful. Life can be summed up and tied together. Death can become the final act of healing.

For another thing, hospital care is expensive. Some other kind of setting is needed to keep the costs of care manageable. For that as well as the other reasons given above, there is more and more interest in making hospice care available. In fact home health agencies such as visiting nurse associations have been giving nursing care to dying persons at home for many years. Friends and neighbors have rallied to help families care for dying persons. The new thing is the deliberate mobilization and coordination of the interdisciplinary team, the selection and training of volunteers, and in some cases the building of special places which enable persons to live out their lives in a homelike environment.

Procuring Hospice Care

How can you secure such help when it is needed? Ask your physician if such a program is available in your community. Raise the question with your pastor, parish priest, or rabbi. If your hospital has a social-service department or a chaplain, they may guide you in finding such a place. In some communities hospices may have been in operation only a short time so that they may not be well-known to the general population. Other communities may be only in the process of organizing them.

The federal government has funded several pilot programs in different settings to test their value and to determine policies about funding them. In 1974 a three-year grant was awarded to the hospice of New Haven, Connecticut to develop a demonstration program of home care for cancer patients. This hospice finally opened a new separate building in 1980. The National Cancer Institute in 1978 awarded contracts to Riverside Hospice in New Jersey, Hill Haven Hospice in Tucson, and Kaiser Permanenta Hospice near Los Angeles as experiments. There is a National Hospice organization with offices in Washington, D.C. The local Cancer Society may also be a source of information and assistance.

Hospice care may be paid for by some insurance company hospitalization policies such as Blue Cross, Medicare, and Medicaid, and by some funded programs such as those which provide homemaker services to persons who qualify. But this needs to be checked out in each case. Policies are changing constantly. When a patient has been referred to a hospice organization by a physician, social worker, clergy, or friends, an assessment of the patient's needs will be made to ascertain if hospice care is appropriate. At that time provision for payment, if any, will be worked out and the program of care planned.

To Die at Home or Not

If our illness has been diagnosed with certainty as terminal within a foreseeable future of months, weeks, or days, under what circumstances would we decide to die at home? Would we prefer to be there or at the hospital? Where would it be better for us to be?

The first condition to consider, I suspect, would be our relationship with the members of our family, particularly those who would be sharing our last days with us and carrying the burden of any care. If our relationship has been close and meaningful and if family ties are still strong, all concerned might want to spend the last days together as a family in the home.

The second condition would be our attitude toward death, our ability to talk about it openly and to deal with the prospect of separation. If the family wishes to share the experience and are able to handle their feelings about it, dying at home might be indicated.

The third condition would have to do with the nature of our illness and the kind of care required, as well as the ability of the family to give that kind of care. Here the availability of a hospice program might be crucial, for the hospice exists to enable families to provide the requisite care and to support them in doing it so the burden is not overwhelming.

To those of us who love life, who have much we want to do yet, and who do not want to part from those we love, as well as to those of us who feel guilty about the past and fear the future, the awareness of impending death usually comes as a blow. Our first impulse may be one of disbelief or denial. This may give way to anger and to grief. Then we may seek desperately for a way out, grasping for a miracle or trying to bargain for a longer lease on life. But finally, it is good if we can accept death as a fact to be faced, an experience through which each of us must go. Then we can decide what to do with our remaining days. Then we can take seriously our stewardship of whatever time we have, with each day being a gift to enjoy.

In the Judeo-Christian tradition the concept of the Sabbath holds an important place. In ancient Babylon it was designated as "a time for quieting the heart." It rests upon the conviction that there is a time for desisting from labor, for restoring the body and soul, for recalling and celebrating what has been experienced in the past and for preparing for the future. The Sabbath is a time for reflecting, for ascertaining meanings, for listening to instruction from the Holy One, and for expressing gratitude. It is a time of summing up and putting together.

This concept of the Sabbath applies to the span of life as well as to the weekly divisions of living. The last period of life may be seen as the Sabbath, when all that has gone before is recalled, put in order, and celebrated. It is a time when loose ends are gathered up, when misunderstandings and separations are healed, when failures are acknowledged, and an attempt is made to start over. This is a time for coming to terms with what we have not been able to do and what we pass on unfinished to those who come after. This is a time for healing and making holy, a time for seeing our lives in the context of the Eternal.

Genesis 47-50 record the last days of Israel, as Jacob came to be called. He had come to the time of his death far from home in a foreign land where he had gone to escape famine and to be with his son Joseph and his family. Tired and full of years, knowing he would soon die, he called together his sons and grandsons and their families. To each of them he gave a blessing. This was his spiritual will, his time of summing up, sorting out, and passing on the heritage he had acquired. During this time he made arrangements for his funeral. He gave instructions about where he was to be buried. Having done all this, he died, and his family wept and mourned for the customary 70 days.

The Hebrew patriarchs lived life in full knowledge that they would die and that death might come at any time, for life was hard and dangerous. Knowing that, they prepared for their demise with dignity and reverence. Time spent under the ministry of a hospice, whether the support is given to us in our own homes or in a special residence, can be a time devoted to the celebration of life, a time of becoming whole, a time for breaking bread and drinking of the communion cup in the fellowship of the family. This is the commitment of the hospice movement.

For Further Reading

Statistics

National Council on Aging. *Fact Book on Aging.* 1979.

National Council on Aging. *The Myth and Reality of Aging in America.* 1976.

A study done by the Louis Harris and Associates polling organization.

U.S. Bureau of the Census. *Current Population Reports.*

Up-to-date population and housing statistics, as well as information on living arrangements.

U.S. Department of Health, Education, and Welfare. *Facts About Older Americans.* Publication No. 79-20006. Available from Superintendent of Documents, Government Printing Office, Washington, D.C.

This is brought up-to-date from time to time.

Soldo, Beth J. *America's Elderly in the 1980s*. The Population Reference Bureau, Inc., 1337 Connecticut Ave. N.W., Washington, D.C. 20036. Vol. 35, No. 4. November, 1980.

> An excellent summary.

Family Relationships

Anderson, Margaret J. *Your Aging Parents*. St. Louis: Concordia, 1979.

Arnstein, Helene S. *Getting Along with Your Grown-Up Children*. New York: Evans, 1970.

> Guidelines for closing the generation gap, aimed at middle-aged and older adults.

Howard, Jane. *Families*. New York: Berkley, 1980.

> A sensitive study and reflection on types of family relationships.

Howell, John C. *Senior Adult Family Life*. Nashville: Broadman, 1979.

> Considers types of family life, developmental concerns, experiencing dynamic maturity, living with crises, and handling marriage and family conflicts from a Christian point of view.

Institute of Gerontology. *Living in the Multigeneration Family*. University of Michigan—Wayne State University, 1969.

Lester, Andrew D. and Judith L. *Understanding Aging Parents*. Philadelphia: Westminster, 1980.

Otten, Jane, and Florence Shelley. *When Your Parents Grow Old*. New York: New American Library, 1978.

> Contains chapters on finding help in the community, improving the quality of your parent's life, dealing with dependency, money matters, disease, and behavioral change.

Silverstone, Barbara, and Helen K. Hyman. *You and Your Aging Parent: The Modern Family's Guide to Emotional, Physical, and Financial Problems*. New York: Pantheon, 1977.

Widowhood

Lopata, Helena Z. *Women as Widows: Support Systems*. New York: Elsevier, 1979.

> A study of 1000 in the Chicago area and the difference made by their support systems. Enlightening.

Peterson, James A. *On Being Alone: A Guide for Widowed Persons*. Available free from AARP-NRTA.

Peterson, James A., and Michael L. Briley. *Widows and Widowhood: A Creative Approach to Being Alone*. Piscataway, N.J.: New Century, 1977.

Reese, Mary E. *Moving On: Overcoming the Crises of Widowhood*. Ridgefield, Conn.: Wyden, 1979.

> A practical, helpful book.

General Information

Brickner, Philip W. *Home Health Care for the Aged: How to Help Older People Stay in Their Homes and Out of*

Institutions. New York: Appleton-Century-Crofts, 1978.

Useful ideas on what to look for and what ought to be provided.

Center for Urban Policy Research. *Retirement Communities: For Adults Only.* 1976.

Clurman, David, and Edna L. Hebard. *Condominiums and Cooperatives.* New York: John Wiley and Sons, 1970.

An introduction and reference to the technical and legal aspects.

Consumer Information Center. Pueblo, Col. 81009. *Questions and Answers on Condominiums.* 605H. *Rent or Buy?* 146H. *Wise Home Buying.* 609H.

These and other useful booklets are prepared by various federal agencies. For a catalog or more information write the center or your congressional representative.

Musson, Noverre. *National Directory of Retirement Residences.* 4th ed. New York: Fell, 1982.

National Council on the Aging. *A Guide for Selection of Retirement Housing.*

NARP-NRTA. *Your Retirement Housing Guide.* 1975.

An excellent 40-page summary of the available options and a discussion of reasons for moving, counsel on moving, and how to sell a house. Highly recommended.

Rand McNally. *Guide to Retirement Living.*

A listing of places with descriptions about each region.

Raimy, Eric. *Shared Houses, Shared Lives: The New Extended Families and How They Work*. Los Angeles: J. P. Tarcher, 1979.

A guide to joining or setting up shared housing with sample agreement forms.

Regnis, Ruth. *Everything Tenants Need to Know to Get Their Money's Worth*. New York: McKay, 1974. Out of print.

A handbook for renters.

Scholen, Kenneth and Yung-Ping Chen, eds. *Unlocking Home Equity for the Elderly*. Cambridge, Mass.: Ballinger, 1980.

A somewhat technical discussion of the issues involved.

Smith, Bert K. *Pursuit of Dignity: New Living Alternatives for the Elderly*. Boston: Beacon, 1977.

Tobin, Sheldon S. and Morton A. Lieberman. *Last Home for the Aged: Critical Implications of Institutionalization*. San Francisco: Jossey-Bass, 1976.

A somewhat technical report of a study of the effects of institutionalization with a chapter on the implications for those providing care.

Wagner, Patricia A. and Jan M. McRae, eds. *Back to Basics: Food and Shelter for the Elderly*. Gainesville: Univ. Presses of Florida, 1979.

A professional discussion of the complex issues of housing and care for the elderly.

Coping with Chronic Illness

Duvoisin, Roger C., M.D. *Parkinson's Disease: A Guide for Patient and Family.* New York: Raven Press, 1978.

Mace, Nancy L., and Peter V. Rabins, M.D. *The 36-Hour Day: A Family Guide to Caring for Persons with Alzheimer's Disease, Related Dementing Illnesses and Memory Loss in Later Life.* Baltimore: John Hopkins, 1982.

   Two fairly new books dealing with chronic illnesses which are quite common among older people. A number of support groups concerned with these illnesses now exist.

Hospice

Davidson, Glen W., ed. *Hospice: Development and Administration.* Washington, D.C.: Hemisphere, 1978.

Hamilton, Michael P., and Helen F. Reid. *A Hospice Handbook: A New Way to Care for the Dying.* Grand Rapids: Eerdmans, 1980.

Lack, Sylvia A., and Robert W. Buckingham III. *First American Hospice: Three Years of Home Care.* Hospice Inc. 765 Prospect St., New Haven, Conn. 06511. 1978.

   History of the first three years of this pioneering project and what they have done.

Stoddard, Sandol. *The Hospice Movement: A Better Way of Caring for the Dying.* New York: Random, 1977.

Nursing Homes

Burger, Sarah G., and Martha D'Erasmo. *Living in a Nursing Home: A Guide for Residents, Their Families, and Friends.* New York: Continuum, 1976.

> Has chapters on shopping for a home, making preparations for entry, reactions to placement, and how to get along. Also how to help a patient. Excellent.

Faunce, Frances Avery. *The Nursing Home Visitor: A Handbook.* Nashville: Abingdon, 1969. Out of print.

> Written from the inside by a patient. Gives excellent suggestions on how to make visits meaningful and how to raise the quality of life for patients.

Glasscote, R. M., and others. *Old Folks at Home: A Field Study of Nursing and Board-and-Care-Facilities.* Publication Services Division, American Psychiatric Association. 1700 18th St. N.W., Washington, D.C. 20009. 1976.

> Teams of mental health specialists studied a sample of homes to test popular conceptions and were surprised to discover that the care and quality of life in many were better than they expected.

Nassau, Jean Barron. *Choosing a Nursing Home.* New York: Funk and Wagnalls. 1975. Out of print.

> How to assess one and adjust to living in one.

NRTA. *Selecting a Nursing Home.* Available from local AARP-NRTA chapters or from the national office.

> A leaflet with a list of items to check off.

Directory of Organizations

American Association of Homes for the Aging.
    1050 17th St. N.W., Washington, D.C. 20036

    A national organization of not-for-profit homes. Many states have state chapters. Can provide a directory of all facilities belonging to the association. Most are associated with religious or service organizations.

American Health Association
    1200 15th St. N.W., Washington, D.C. 20005

    An organization of proprietary (80%) and non-proprietary long-term health care facilities with state chapters.

Gerontology Society of America
    1835 K St. N.W., Suite 305, Washington D.C. 20006

    An association of professionals in the field of aging focusing mainly on research. Publishes the *Journal of Gerontology*, reporting on research and *The Gerontologist*, which often contains articles on housing, health care, and national policy. The *Journal of Gerontology* indexes all publications in the field of aging.

Human Development Services
U.S. Department of Health and Human Services

Publishes the magazine entitled *Aging,* which is an organ of the department but which often carries articles on housing, living arrangements, and governmental policies.

National Council on the Aging, Inc.
1826 L Street N.W., Washington, D.C. 20036

A national organization seeking to coordinate and stimulate research, training, and service in the field of aging and to act as advocate for the aging. Sponsors research and publishes timely material.

National Retired Teachers Association and the American Association of Retired Persons
1909 K St. N.W., Washington, D.C. 20049

Maintains local chapters and regional offices in addition to the national office, supports research, acts as advocate for the elderly, and publishes a number of extremely helpful pamphlets as well as the magazine *Mature Years.*

Share-A-Home Association
43 Gay Dr., Winter Park, Fla. 32789

Can provide information on existing groups working in this area.

Western Gerontological Society
785 Market St., Suite 1114, San Francisco, Cal. 94103

An association of professionals with more of a slant

toward the practitioner and older people themselves. Publishes *Generations,* which often carries both news and analyses of issues in the field of aging, including those of housing, living arrangements, and income maintenance.